Concise Answers to

Frequently Asked Questions

About Professional Learning
Communities at Work®

Mike Mattos

Richard DuFour

Rebecca DuFour

Robert Eaker

Thomas W. Many

Solution Tree | Press

a division of
Solution Tree

555 North Morton Street
Bloomington, IN 47404
800.733.6786 (toll free) / 812.336.7700
FAX: 812.336.7790

email: info@SolutionTree.com
SolutionTree.com

Visit **go.SolutionTree.com/PLCbooks** to access materials related to this book.

Printed in the United States of America

Library of Congress Cataloging-in-Publication Data

Names: Mattos, Mike (Mike William)
Title: Concise answers to frequently asked questions about professional
   learning communities at work / Mike Mattos, Richard DuFour, Rebecca
   DuFour, Robert Eaker, Thomas W. Many.
Description: Bloomington, IN : Solution Tree Press, [2016] | "Designed to be
   a companion guidebook for book Learning by Doing: A Handbook for
   Professional Learning Communities at Work (3rd ed.)" | Includes
   bibliographical references and index.
Identifiers: LCCN 2016007626 | ISBN 9781942496632 (perfect bound)
Subjects: LCSH: Professional learning communities. | Teachers--In-service
   training.
Classification: LCC LB1731 .M395 2016 | DDC 370.71/1--dc23 LC record available at http://
lccn.loc.gov/2016007626

Solution Tree
Jeffrey C. Jones, CEO
Edmund M. Ackerman, President

Solution Tree Press
President: Douglas M. Rife
Editorial Director: Tonya Maddox Cupp
Senior Acquisitions Editor: Amy Rubenstein
Managing Production Editor: Caroline Weiss
Senior Production Editor: Suzanne Kraszewski
Copy Editor: Miranda Addonizio
Proofreader: Jessi Finn
Cover and Text Designer: Rian Anderson

To my mentor and dear friend Rick DuFour: words fail to capture the depth and breadth of your impact on my life. I am forever grateful.

—Mike Mattos

To my mother, Colleen Vanness, who at ninety years old has proven there is no age limit on experiencing joy.

—Rick DuFour

To my husband, Rick DuFour, who is proving that cancer is not the winner. So blessed to be your wife, partner, and soul mate!

—Becky DuFour

For my beautiful daughters, Robin and Carrie, and my wonderful grandchildren, Wyatt and Emma.

—Bob Eaker

To all those who continue to ask questions and seek answers about our work; my past and present colleagues in District 96; the associates at Solution Tree; my wife, Susan; and my coauthors, Mike, Bob, Becky, and most especially, Rick.

—Tom Many

Acknowledgments

The Professional Learning Communities at Work® process is, in effect, sweeping the globe. No one has played a greater role in making this possible than Jeffrey Jones, the CEO of Solution Tree. Jeff has been a staunch advocate of our work, a truly visionary leader, and a dear friend. We also thank Solution Tree Press president Douglas M. Rife and his talented staff for bringing this book from concept to completion. Suzanne Kraszewski did a superb job editing our manuscript, and Rian Anderson created a dynamic cover and text design. We hope that this book moves Solution Tree one step closer to achieving its vision of transforming education worldwide to ensure learning for all.

We would also like to thank our family of PLC at Work associates. The answers this book provides are based on the experiences of outstanding educators who have led the PLC process in their own schools and districts. They have blazed a trail for others to follow, gaining wisdom and insight that can only be earned by actually doing the work and achieving unprecedented levels of learning for students. Most important, they generously share this knowledge with others.

Visit **go.SolutionTree.com/PLCbooks** to access materials related to this book.

Table of Contents

Chapter 2

Fostering a Collaborative Culture 37

Forming Teams. 38

Chapter 3

What Do We Want Our Students to Learn?..75

Chapter 4

How Will We Know When Our Students Have Learned It?

Chapter 5
How Will We Respond When Some Students Don't Learn and When Some Do?

Chapter 6

Defining the District's Role in the PLC Process

Chapter 7

Addressing Consensus and Conflict in a PLC

About the Authors

Mike Mattos is an internationally recognized author, presenter, and practitioner who specializes in uniting teachers, administrators, and support staff to transform schools by implementing the response to intervention (RTI) and PLC processes. Mike co-created the RTI at Work™ model, which builds on the foundation of the PLC at Work process to successfully create systematic, multitiered systems of support to ensure high levels of learning for all students.

He is former principal of Marjorie Veeh Elementary School and Pioneer Middle School in California. At both schools, Mike helped create powerful PLCs, improving learning for all students. In 2004, Marjorie Veeh, an elementary school with a large population of youth at risk, won the California Distinguished School and National Title I Achieving School awards.

A National Blue Ribbon School, Pioneer is among only thirteen schools in the United States selected by the GE Foundation as a Best-Practice Partner and is one of eight schools chosen by Richard DuFour to be featured in the video series *The Power of Professional Learning Communities at Work®: Bringing the Big Ideas to Life*. Based on standardized test scores, Pioneer ranks among the top 1 percent of California secondary schools and, in 2009 and 2011, was named Orange County's top middle school. For his leadership, Mike was named the Orange County Middle School Administrator of the Year by the Association of California School Administrators.

To learn more about Mike's work, visit AllThingsPLC (www.allthingsPLC.info), and follow him on Twitter @mikemattos65.

Richard DuFour, EdD, was a public school educator for thirty-four years, serving as a teacher, principal, and superintendent. During his nineteen-year tenure as a leader at Adlai E. Stevenson High School in Lincolnshire, Illinois, Stevenson was one of only three schools in the United States to win the U.S. Department of Education Blue Ribbon Award on four occasions and the first comprehensive high school to be designated a New America High School as a model of successful school reform. He received his state's highest award as both a principal and superintendent.

A prolific author and sought-after consultant, Dr. DuFour is recognized as one of the leading authorities on helping school practitioners implement the PLC at Work process in their schools and districts.

Dr. DuFour was presented the Distinguished Scholar Practitioner Award from the University of Illinois and was the 2004 recipient of the National Staff Development Council's Distinguished Service Award.

To learn more about Dr. DuFour's work, visit AllThingsPLC (www.allthingsPLC .info).

Rebecca DuFour has served as a teacher, school administrator, and central office coordinator. As a former elementary principal, she helped her school earn state and national recognition as a model PLC. She is coauthor of numerous books, articles, and a video series on the topic of PLCs.

Serving as a consultant for more than fifteen years, Becky brings more than thirty-five years of professional experience to her work with educators around the world who are implementing the PLC process in their own organizations.

Becky is the recipient of the Distinguished Alumni Award of Lynchburg College.

To learn more about Becky's work, visit AllThingsPLC (www.allthingsPLC.info).

Robert Eaker, EdD, is professor emeritus at Middle Tennessee State University, where he also served as dean of the College of Education and interim vice president and provost. Dr. Eaker is a former fellow with the National Center for Effective Schools Research and Development. He has written widely on the issues of effective teaching, effective schools, helping teachers use research findings, and high expectations for student achievement. Dr. Eaker was instrumental in the founding of the Tennessee Teachers Hall of Fame and was a regular contributor to the Effective Schools Research Abstracts series.

To learn more about Dr. Eaker's work, visit AllThingsPLC (www.allthingsPLC .info).

Thomas W. Many, EdD, works with teachers, administrators, school boards, parents, and other education stakeholders on organizational leadership, implementation and change, and PLC at Work strategies and concepts.

Dr. Many's long and distinguished career includes twenty years of experience as a superintendent. He has also served as a classroom teacher, learning center director, curriculum supervisor, principal, and assistant superintendent.

As former superintendent of Kildeer Countryside Community Consolidated School District 96 in Illinois, Dr. Many used the tenets of the PLC at Work process to ensure high levels of learning for all students. He played a key role in preparing elementary and middle-grade students to enter Adlai E. Stevenson High School, a nationally recognized PLC. Under Dr. Many's leadership, student achievement in District 96 improved every year for twelve consecutive years. More than 95 percent of all students now meet or exceed state standards. The district has been especially effective in helping students with special needs improve their academic performance. It has become recognized as one of the premier elementary school districts in the United States. A dedicated PLC practitioner, he is a compelling and sought-after speaker.

Dr. Many has written numerous articles and has coauthored books.

To learn more about Dr. Many's work, visit AllThingsPLC (www.allthingsPLC .info).

To book Mike Mattos, Richard DuFour, Rebecca DuFour, Robert Eaker, or Thomas W. Many for professional development, contact pd@SolutionTree.com.

Introduction

Remodeling Your School: The Unexpected Obstacles

Have you ever experienced a major home remodeling project or known someone who has? We don't mean something minor, like repainting a bedroom or installing new kitchen countertops. We mean demolition, redesigning, and rebuilding; you can't recognize it when you're done; you could have been on a home-improvement television show with this kind of remodeling. If you have ever taken on such a project—and lived to tell the tale—then you probably gained a greater understanding of the well-known line from Robert Burns's poetry, "The best-laid plans of mice and men often go awry."

It seems no amount of planning can totally prepare you for a job of this magnitude. Before starting the project, you can do everything within your power to prepare; you can visit model homes for ideas, read books on remodeling, select an experienced architect to create detailed plans, receive city approval for the blueprints, and hire a highly recommended general contractor to carry out the work. Without question, this groundwork is vital. Yet, despite all your planning, once you actually start the work, you will face unforeseen questions and obstacles. Some problems will be easy to fix, and others could stop construction in its tracks. When embarking on any project of this scope, it would be naïve to think that everything will run smoothly from start to finish. In the end, navigating the unforeseen obstacles is the key to ultimate success.

Becoming a professional learning community (PLC) is no different. Before beginning your school's PLC journey, you can read books on the topic, attend conferences, visit model schools, and hire experienced consultants to provide professional development; you can do everything within your power to plan for success. While such careful preparation is necessary prior to asking educators to commit to the PLC process, this groundwork alone will not be enough. PLC practices do not represent minor tweaks to our traditional school system; they involve demolition, redesigning, and rebuilding, and you can't recognize it when you're done. If there was a home-improvement television show for education, transformation into a PLC would be a featured makeover. Questions will arise and hurdles will emerge once you actually start doing the work. Some questions will be minor, like how often collaborative teacher teams should give common formative assessments. Other obstacles can bring the entire process to a screeching halt, such as how we will create time for frequent collaboration. How you address the unexpected will ultimately determine if your efforts to become a PLC will be a successful remodeling or a disastrous re-muddling.

A Sequential, Nonlinear, and Cyclical Process

Remodeling a house is a very sequential and linear process. When building an addition, for example, the foundation must be poured before framing can begin. Framing the walls precedes installing the windows. Each step is clearly defined and follows a logical construction process. But becoming a PLC is different; it is a sequential process, but it is also cyclical and nonlinear. (We know—being both sequential and nonlinear sounds like an oxymoron.) You see, there are practices in the PLC process that do have a logical, step-by-step design. For example, take the four critical questions that guide the work of teacher teams.

1. What do we want students to know and be able to do?

2. How will we know when they have learned it?

3. What will we do when they haven't learned it?

4. What will we do to extend the learning when they already know it?

Teacher teams must address these questions sequentially. It would be difficult for a teacher team to create a common assessment to determine if students are learning if the team skipped the first critical question and did not identify what they expect their students to learn in the first place. Likewise, it would be difficult to respond when students don't learn if there was no assessment process designed to measure student progress.

Yet, due to unforeseen bumps in the road—the obstacles you encounter once you begin actually doing the work of becoming a PLC—you will most assuredly have to backtrack sometimes before you can move forward. Continuing with our example, it is not uncommon for teacher teams to initially answer critical question one by identifying a list of power standards from the required state curriculum. When the team then turns to the second critical question, members will likely find it difficult to create a common assessment if they have not unpacked the standard to ensure team members have defined the standard the same way, agreed on the rigor level students must reach to demonstrate proficiency, and settled on the scope and sequence of when each standard will be taught. Seeing that they can't answer the second critical question without this additional information, the team members would need to go back to the first question before creating their common assessment. The process is sequential in design yet nonlinear in actual implementation.

Using the same example, we can see how the PLC process is also cyclical. A collaborative teacher team will likely apply the four critical questions when planning for their first unit of the school year. The team will:

- Clarify the essential skills and concepts embedded in the unit

- Design a common formative assessment to administer at the end of the unit

- Teach the unit within the agreed-on window of time, according to the team's common pacing guide

- Give the common assessment

- Collectively review the results to reflect on their individual and collective teaching and identify students who need additional time and support to learn the essential curriculum

- Provide interventions and extension

When it is done, what will the team do next? They repeat the process for the next unit of study. But in the next unit, the team will have learned the importance of unpacking standards when answering the first critical question, so backtracking will be less likely. This is what the PLC process is designed to do: create continuous, job-embedded adult learning to improve student achievement. You learn most often when you encounter obstacles and then find better ways to overcome and move forward. But if a team gets stuck and can't overcome the unexpected, the process gets bogged down, and learning stops.

Your Guide on the Side

The purpose of this book is to be your "guide on the side" when you have specific questions or encounter obstacles on your journey to becoming a PLC. There is an old Chinese proverb that advises, "To know the road ahead, ask those coming back." The essential elements of the PLC process are firmly grounded in powerful research, but we have honed and refined the process through our work as site educators. We refer to our process as PLC at Work because we are not theorists; we are practitioners. Before writing their first book on PLCs, Rick DuFour and Bob Eaker worked together for more than twenty years. Along with the dedicated staff at Adlai E. Stevenson High School in Lincolnshire, Illinois, they learned about the most proven practices to increase student learning, started applying them, faced obstacles, tried again, and found solutions. Tom Many's district, Kildeer Countryside Community Consolidated School District 96, fed into Stevenson, and he joined Rick and Bob on the journey. Becky DuFour and Mike Mattos learned from Rick and Bob about the PLC process, began the journey at their own elementary and middle schools, hit bumps along the way, and ultimately worked with their staff members to overcome the obstacles and succeed. Since the mid-1990s, we have helped thousands of educators across the globe successfully remodel their schools into PLCs. During the panel discussions at PLC at Work Institutes, we have been asked hundreds of questions about the process we have and assisted educators in exploring and resolving those questions.

These experiences allow us to anticipate the questions you will have along the way, identify the likely obstacles you will face, and provide the answers and advice you need to move forward.

How This Book Is Organized

Concise Answers to Frequently Asked Questions About Professional Learning Communities at Work is designed as a companion to *Learning by Doing: A Handbook for Professional Learning Communities at Work, Third Edition* (DuFour, DuFour, Eaker, Many, & Mattos, 2016). *Learning by Doing* is a detailed road map for exactly how to become a PLC. It digs deeply into each essential element of the PLC process, cites comprehensive research supporting every practice, outlines specific implementation steps, offers relevant case studies, and provides sample products and targeted rubrics to assess your progress. Without question, it is a must-have resource for any organization committed to becoming a PLC.

Concise Answers to Frequently Asked Questions is your simplified, quick-reference guide on the side to PLCs. Our goals with this book are to provide:

- **Succinct answers to frequently asked questions**—Think about a time when you bought a new electronic device for your home, like a flat-screen television. The device probably came with two sets of directions—one set a comprehensive review of the entire product, explaining every relevant detail and feature, and the other set a more concise, quick-reference guide. The latter is not designed to answer every question in complete detail, but instead to provide brief answers to very specific, timely questions. Both have similar content but are designed to assist the user in different ways. *Learning by Doing, Third Edition*, is the comprehensive manual. It is designed to provide in-depth research and information on every aspect of the PLC process. *Concise Answers to Frequently Asked Questions* is your quick-reference guide. In it, we have identified the most frequently asked questions and common obstacles that schools face when becoming a PLC and then provided concise, targeted answers.

- **Quick access**—This book is designed so the reader can easily navigate to a specific answer without having to read an entire chapter for the information. The detailed table of contents contains both the larger chapter topics and the specific questions addressed in each area. If a teacher team is working on the first critical question, for example, and wants to know how many essential standards they should identify, they can quickly turn to chapter 3 (titled "What Do We Want Our Students to Learn?") and look up the question, "How many essential standards should teacher teams select?" The team does not have to read the entire chapter, only the answer to their specific question.

- **Simple language**—*Learning by Doing, Third Edition*, is written in a very clear and understandable style. But because one of the book's goals is to provide comprehensive evidence supporting each PLC practice, it cites a significant amount of research, which includes some academic language. *Concise Answers to Frequently Asked Questions* assumes readers do not need to be convinced to become a PLC. Subsequently, we give less attention to citing research, allowing us to purposefully write straight-to-the-point answers using candid, common-sense language.

We envision schools relying on both resources, *Learning by Doing, Third Edition*, and *Concise Answers to Frequently Asked Questions*, throughout their PLC journey. The former is an excellent resource at the beginning to build understanding and clarity on the overall process and as a tool to use on an ongoing basis when a deeper review of each element of the PLC process is necessary. *Concise Answers to Frequently Asked Questions* is a timely reference resource to use when specific questions and unexpected obstacles arise.

PLCs 101

While many readers of this book might already have prior knowledge of the basic elements of the PLC process, we expect that some readers are learning about the model for the first time. To use this book most effectively, you should understand some fundamental PLC vocabulary.

What is a PLC?

The official definition of a professional learning community is "an ongoing process in which educators work collaboratively in recurring cycles of collective inquiry and action research to achieve better results for the students they serve" (DuFour, DuFour, Eaker, & Many, 2010, p. 11). More simply stated, the PLC process is a never-ending process in which educators commit to working together to ensure higher levels of learning for every student. They achieve this outcome by learning together about the best practices proven to increase student learning, applying what they have learned, and using evidence of student learning to make decisions and revisions in practice to help even more students learn at higher levels.

What is the PLC—the entire district, the school, or the individual teams within the school?

The larger organization is the PLC. So if a district has committed to the PLC process, then the district is considered a PLC. If a single school within a district has committed to the PLC process, then the school is considered the PLC. Within each PLC, teachers form collaborative teams to best achieve the mission of ensuring high levels of learning for all. While collaborative teacher teams are part of the larger PLC, we do not refer to each teacher team as a PLC.

What is collective inquiry?

Collective inquiry means learning together. In a PLC, we do not make decisions by averaging opinions, guessing, or defaulting to "This is how we have always done it." We are professional educators. The very definition of a profession is a job that requires specialized education, training, or skill and that includes the use of accepted best practices. Members of a profession are expected to know and apply these practices on behalf of their clients—in this case, students. Because education research continues to grow and evolve, educators within a school must learn continuously to achieve higher levels of learning for students.

What is action research?

Research alone cannot improve student learning; you must turn research into action. Action research means we apply what we have learned. We try it out, in our own school or district and with our own students. In a PLC, we are willing to try new practices and procedures and then measure their impact on student learning to determine if the change was beneficial.

What are the three big ideas?

Becoming a PLC is a process; it is not a program to simply put in place. Three guiding principles, the *three big ideas*, steer the process. They are:

1. A focus on learning

2. A collaborative culture

3. A results orientation

The more a school or district can align its practices and procedures to these ideas, the higher the probability that it functions as a PLC, and, more important, the more its students will learn.

What is a focus on learning?

A focus on learning is a PLC's commitment to making student learning the fundamental purpose of the school or district. This means that you assess every policy, practice, and procedure with these questions: Will doing this lead to higher levels of learning for our students? Are we willing to revise or discontinue actions that fail to increase student learning?

What is a collaborative culture?

Because no single educator has all the time, skills, and knowledge to ensure all students learn at high levels, educators in a PLC school or district commit to working collaboratively to achieve this outcome. Working collaboratively is neither optional nor invitational; every member of the organization is expected to work as part of a collaborative team. Equally important, the organization dedicates the time and resources necessary to make collaboration job embedded.

What is a results orientation?

It is commonly said that the road to hell is paved with good intentions. In a PLC, we acknowledge that acting on our good intentions to help students is not enough; we must know if our actions actually lead to higher levels of learning. A PLC purposefully seeks timely, relevant information—evidence of student learning—that confirms which practices are increasing student learning and which actions are not.

What is a culture that is simultaneously loose and tight?

A culture that is simultaneously loose and tight is one that empowers people to make important decisions and encourages them to be creative and innovative (loose), while at the same time, demands that certain aspects of the culture are nondiscretionary and required (tight).

In a PLC, the tight aspects include the following.

- Educators work collaboratively rather than in isolation and have clarified the commitments they make to each other about how they will work together.

- The fundamental structure of the school becomes the collaborative team in which members work interdependently to achieve common goals for which all members are mutually accountable.

- The team establishes a guaranteed curriculum, unit by unit, so all students have access to the same knowledge and skills regardless of which teacher they are assigned.

- The team develops common formative assessments to frequently gather evidence of student learning.

- The school has created systems of intervention to ensure students who struggle receive additional time and support for learning in a way that is timely, directive, diagnostic, and systematic.

- The team uses evidence of student learning to inform and improve the individual and collective practice of the team members.

The loose aspects of the culture include empowering teams to establish their own goals, collective commitments, guaranteed and viable curriculum, pacing, instructional practices, common assessments, and schoolwide system of interventions. In other words, educators are given the authority to make very important decisions in a PLC, but, in return, they must be willing to accept responsibility for the outcomes of those decisions and committed to improving the results they are experiencing.

The PLC process requires a culture that is simultaneously loose and tight on the right work.

We have had meetings at our school for years, so are we a PLC?

Being a PLC is more than just meeting together as a faculty, with grade-level colleagues, and in departments. In a PLC, collaboration requires taking collective responsibility for student learning and working interdependently to achieve this outcome. To guide this process, the collaboration centers on four critical questions.

1. What do we want students to know and be able to do?

2. How will we know when they have learned it?

3. What will we do when they haven't learned it?

4. What will we do to extend the learning when they already know it?

Why are the three big ideas so important to the PLC process?

We cannot overemphasize the importance of the three big ideas to the PLC process. When educators truly embrace and act on these ideas, the answers to many of the inevitable questions that arise in PLC transformation become evident. Imagine a school in which the educators have built consensus on the following assertions.

"We recognize that the fundamental purpose of our school and the reason we come to work each day is to ensure all students learn at high levels. We understand that helping all students learn requires a collective, collaborative effort rather than a series of isolated efforts. Therefore, we work in teams and constantly gather evidence of student learning for two purposes: to inform and improve our individual and collective practice and to better meet the needs of individual students through intervention or extension."

Without this shared understanding of basic assumptions, every question that arises in a school can become a matter for debate based on individual opinions and personal war stories. When others accept these assumptions, they serve as filters that guide the decision-making process in a PLC. So recognize that while this book offers responses to discrete questions, it is also intended to help you answer virtually any question by giving you insight into how members of a PLC think.

A Word of Caution

It is important that you use this book correctly: as a powerful reference guide to help you along during your PLC journey. Becoming a PLC requires a deep understanding of the essential elements of the PLC process. Additionally, as a PLC identifies areas of need—such as better grading practices that are proven to increase student motivation and achievement—it digs deeply to identify best next steps. This book is not intended to be the CliffsNotes of the PLC process, providing shortcuts to the right answers. Those who use this book wisely will gain timely insight and clarity on specific steps on the PLC journey from educators who have traveled the same path, as in the old proverb. Those who do not will learn a valuable lesson: there are no shortcuts on the journey to becoming a PLC. This book is designed to quicken your pace, not to help you skip steps.

Chapter 1

Laying the Foundation: Mission, Vision, Values, and Goals

Becky's brother, Russ, has been a building contractor in the Central Virginia area for more than thirty-six years. Over the course of his career, Russ and his team have built some beautiful residential and commercial structures of various styles and sizes. All of Russ's projects—even the smallest structures—start with the crew laying a solid foundation on which the structure will stand. A building contractor who neglects to lay a solid foundation would be foolish at best and vulnerable to a lawsuit at worst. The lack of a solid foundation may not be apparent at first, especially to someone not involved in the building project, but it won't be long before the structure will begin to leak, crack, settle, and ultimately tumble down.

Educational leaders committed to building high-performing PLCs that will withstand the test of time must establish a strong foundation before expecting educators to embrace the new and different work that drives continuous cycles of improvement in a PLC. Leaders do this by engaging members of the school and district community to consider the questions posed by the four pillars that represent that foundation of a PLC. See figure 1.1 (page 12).

The four pillars of the structure in figure 1.1—shared mission, shared vision, collective commitments, and shared goals—constitute the solid foundation of a PLC. Once the shared foundation is in place, future proposed changes in structure and culture will be considered through the lens of whether the proposed change is aligned with promoting and protecting the shared foundation. This foundation supports the learning-focused work of collaborative teams and the vertical dialogue that takes place between teams. We will elaborate on the collaborative culture of a PLC in chapter 2. In this chapter, we provide more clarity about the importance of addressing each of the four pillars and answer frequently asked questions about them.

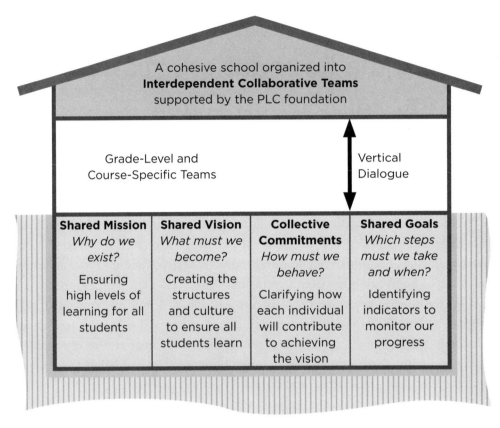

Figure 1.1: The PLC structure.

Mission

What is a school's mission?

The mission pillar answers the question, Why do we exist? In a PLC, the mission—the fundamental purpose of the school—is to ensure high levels of learning for all, students and staff alike. This collective purpose sets the direction for the organization and serves as a compass to guide its actions.

Are the mission and a school's mission statement the same thing?

Although the mission—the fundamental purpose—of a PLC is to ensure high levels of learning for all, a school's mission statement might include different language or expand on that ideal. A well-articulated mission statement answers the question, Why do we exist? Regardless of the verbiage, the notion that all members of the school's community will learn at high levels is evident. The challenge confronting educators

in every school is to align their actual practices and procedures with the words of
their mission statement.

How long should a mission statement be?

Most mission statements involve three or four sentences that expand on the idea
that the fundamental purpose of the school is to ensure high levels of learning for all.
When a mission statement becomes too long for most people to commit to memory,
the school community may embrace a motto that captures the essence of the mission
statement. Examples of school mottoes include "Learning for All," "Success for All,"
and "Hand in Hand, We All Learn."

What is a learning-focused mission?

As educators, are we here to teach and cover a curriculum, or are we here to ensure
students actually learn the curriculum? A learning-focused mission assumes that our
schools were not built so educators have a place to teach, but instead so students have
a place to learn. In the PLC process, the first big idea, a focus on learning, captures
this belief. The fundamental purpose of a PLC is to ensure high levels of learning for
every student.

The PLC process is a way of thinking. Getting educators to shift from a mindset
of teaching, covering material, ranking, and sorting to learning for all is a difficult
task. Once a school embraces this mission and understands the new lenses through
which one must view the work, traditional practices that are counterproductive to
this goal become apparent.

Think of this shift in mindset as similar to the experience of looking at an optical
illusion graphic. First, you see the obvious picture, like a beach scene, but after you
examine the image long enough, you start to view it another way. A new picture
emerges of an elephant in a clown car. Once you get it, you think, "How did I miss
that elephant?" Until you mastered the ability to look at the picture with the correct
gaze, it really did look like a traditional beach scene. That is what the shift from a
teaching focus to a learning focus is like.

What does *high levels of learning* mean?

We define *high levels of learning* as "high school plus," meaning every child is on
a trajectory to graduate from high school with the academic skills, knowledge, and
dispositions needed to continue to learn. A high school diploma will not be enough
to compete in the global marketplace and make a living. Postsecondary education can

include attending a university, community college, trade school, internship, apprenticeship, or some other type of specialized training.

To achieve this, all students must learn at grade level or better every year. For example, a first grader who ends the year unprepared for second grade is at risk of ultimately not graduating from high school, let alone successfully transitioning to postsecondary levels of education. A school focused on high levels of learning would not allow students to be tracked in below-grade-level learning.

Does *all* really mean all?

Without question, committing to a mission of high levels of learning for all students is a daunting task. But if a school settles for less—that *most* students will learn at high levels—then how does the school determine which students deserve a substandard education and diminished opportunities in life? How many failing students would such a school deem acceptable? Once a school falters on its commitment to high levels of learning for every student, it starts down a slippery slope of lowering expectations for some students.

Isn't it unrealistic to expect all students to learn at high levels?

A frequent concern raised when committing to all students learning at high levels is this: Aren't some students born with a greater aptitude to succeed? If this premise is true, then how does a school accurately determine which students are born to academically thrive, and which are not? There is a harsh reality that we, as educators, must address if we ever hope to reach our mission of learning for all: most schools have been inaccurately and unfairly judging student academic potential, to the detriment of our most at-risk youth. Research proves that schools are far more likely to place students in lower tracks of learning and identify them for special education if they come from a home of poverty, are minorities, are males, and are non-native English speakers. And conversely, schools are much less likely to deem the same population "gifted" and place them in an advanced-level curriculum.

This reality raises critical questions for any school dedicated to a mission of learning for all. Are minority students born with a diminished capacity to learn at high levels? Does learning any language besides English at birth genetically alter a student's ability to learn at high levels? Does poverty irreversibly ruin a student's potential to learn? Of course not! A student's native language and economic status do not reduce the student's innate capacity to learn, although they may make it more challenging for educators to ensure that learning. Yet these misconceptions based on a student's demographics become a self-fulfilling prophecy. Educators place the students they perceive as capable of learning at high levels in more rigorous coursework, teach them at advanced levels, and expect them to achieve; they are thus much more likely to learn at a higher level. But they place the students they perceive as less capable of learning at high levels in below-grade-level curriculum, teach them at remedial levels, and expect them to achieve at lower levels, and, to no one's surprise, these students will most likely learn at low levels.

We are not against differentiated instruction, but it is the teaching methods that are differentiated, not the student expectations. In other words, the third-grade team should determine the essential standards for all third graders and what it will look like if a child is proficient (the rigor level). This is the expectation for all students. If students are grouped to meet this standard, that is fine. Just be careful—what most schools call differentiation is really tracking. Often students placed in the low group get "modified curriculum"—code for remedial, watered-down expectations. If our mission is for all students to learn at high levels, we must teach all students at high levels.

Any school dedicated to a mission of high levels of learning for all must assume that all students are capable of achieving the outcome. In the end, it is possible that some students may not achieve this outcome in spite of all the collaborative efforts of the school. But if a school begins the process by assuming some students won't succeed, then most assuredly some will not.

If we make our mission high levels of learning for every child, what about students in special education?

At some schools, there is a very small percentage of students who have such severe disabilities that it may be virtually impossible for them to reach the standard of high school plus. If a school has determined beyond a shadow of a doubt that a student has profound disabilities, and will assuredly be incapable of living independently as an adult, it would be appropriate to modify that student's learning outcomes to better prepare the student for the needs of his or her unique adult life. But a vast majority of students identified for special education will be independent adults. They will not receive "modified" rent or "accommodated" bills—just as with English learners, children of poverty, and students who come from home environments that are counterproductive to success in school. These students must learn at high levels. With the rare exception for students who are severely disabled, all really must mean all.

Isn't it a school's job to give students the opportunity to learn—not to ensure they learn?

There are those who suggest that the purpose of schooling is not to ensure students learn but merely to give them the opportunity to learn. This premise is reflected in the mantra, "It is our job to teach; it is their job to learn." This approach absolves educators of any responsibility for students who are unsuccessful in the K–12 setting. From this perspective, students who choose to live in conditions that are not conducive to learning—high poverty, families that are unable or unwilling to support their learning, no positive role models—should suffer the consequences of their circumstances. This premise allows schools to simply serve as a sorting and selecting mechanism. Schools allow students without certain innate abilities and dispositions to fail and, ultimately, withdraw from the educational system. Of course, those who do will earn thirty-three cents for every dollar a college graduate makes and sixty-six cents for every dollar a high school graduate makes, have a life expectancy that is ten to thirteen years shorter than a college graduate's, have an unemployment rate that is five times higher than those with post–high school education, be far more likely to live in poverty, and have only a one in seventeen chance of their own children ever attending college. Each high school dropout will cost society more than $250,000 in lost taxes, be involved in higher rates of criminal activity, and have a higher reliance on Medicaid and welfare benefits over his or her lifetime (Stark, Noel, & McFarland, 2015).

Schools must do more than teach and test and hope for the best. The consequences for failure in the K–12 system have never been more dire. Educators have a moral imperative to do everything they can to ensure high levels of learning for all students. Members of our profession cannot be indifferent to whether students learn.

What is the student's responsibility in his or her learning?

Educators would certainly prefer that each student who enters their schools is blessed with an innate sense of self-discipline, diligence, work ethic, time management, and other qualities that might come under the general heading of "responsibility." Alas, some students are not innately responsible and, in fact, are highly irresponsible. The question facing schools is, How can we teach our irresponsible students to become more responsible?

A long-standing tradition in our profession is to simply allow irresponsible students to fail. Advocates of this position argue that if students fail to study, fail to complete their work, fail to put in the necessary time to become proficient, or fail to meet deadlines, they should suffer the logical consequence of their actions—failure. Failure will teach the students the errors of their ways, enlighten them, and cause them to act more responsibly in the future. The tradition persists despite the fact that more than a century of evidence shows that it does not work. Anyone who has ever taught should be willing to acknowledge that if students are told, "You must do this work at a high level of quality and turn it in on time, or you will fail," some students will be perfectly content to fail. Allowing them the option of not doing the work merely reinforces their irresponsibility.

A school that allows irresponsible students to elect to fail by not completing assignments or putting forth the effort necessary to learn does not teach students to act responsibly. In fact, it is counterintuitive to suggest that allowing an irresponsible student to choose to act irresponsibly teaches responsibility.

Schools that are committed to providing students with essential knowledge, skills, and dispositions (including responsibility) put systems in place to hold students accountable for doing what responsible people do—and responsible people do the work. These schools monitor each student's progress closely and implement structures that require students to do what is necessary to succeed. They provide incentives for completing work on time and consequences for failing to meet deadlines or not achieving the acceptable standard of work. What they do not do is absolve the student of the responsibility of doing the work. The best schools bombard students with the message, "We will not let you off the hook. We will see to it that you do what is necessary to be successful. We won't place you in a less rigorous curriculum, nor will we lower our standards for this course or grade level. We will give you the support, time, and structure to help you be successful, but we will not lower the bar."

It is ironic that educators who insist students should be solely responsible for their own learning define their own jobs in such a way to absolve them of responsibility for seeing to it that students learn.

What is the parents' responsibility for their children's success in school?

Educators committed to helping all students learn at high levels cannot overlook the extensive research base proclaiming the significant impact parents can have on student achievement (Center for Public Education, 2011; Epstein, 2005; U.S. Department of Education, 1995). When parents are involved in their children's education, students achieve more regardless of race or socioeconomic factors. In a perfect world, every parent would embrace this responsibility and would understand how to best fulfill it. There is, however, no reason to believe parents intuitively know how they can best support the learning of their children. Parent involvement increases when schools welcome parents into the teaching and learning process, communicate the importance of the parents' role in student success, and provide explicit strategies for parents to become involved in their children's learning.

Grade-level teams in elementary schools can create concise summaries of essential learning targets, pacing guides, and review materials each month to provide parents with the tools to support student learning at home. Teams can send brief checklist assessments to parents on a weekly basis to get feedback from parents on whether their children are proficient in target skills, are approaching proficiency, or seem to be lost. Teams can model the use of these materials at teacher-parent nights and follow up with phone calls or home visits to any family unable to attend the meeting.

At the secondary school level, parents may feel less comfortable tutoring and assessing the proficiency of their children. They may lack the content expertise and are unlikely to have pedagogical skill. But secondary school parents also benefit from a clear explanation of how they can contribute to the success of their children. In the late 1980s, Adlai E. Stevenson High School in Lincolnshire, Illinois, convened a task force of parents and presented them with the charge of developing research-based strategies for the kind of parental support that would impact student achievement. The recommendations have been sent annually to each parent of a Stevenson student ever since. Adlai E. Stevenson's website (www.d125.org/about/vision/collective -commitments-parents) makes these parent commitments available online.

Most parents want their children to have a great school experience and are willing to help shape that experience. But if educators at all levels hope to forge beneficial partnerships with parents, they must take the initiative to clarify exactly how parents can contribute to the success of their students.

Members of our profession must also recognize that not every parent has the opportunity, time, skill, or interest to become a positive partner in the education of his or her children. The single mother working two jobs to try to keep her family afloat, the father unable to read materials intended to support his child's learning, the mother who does not believe success in education is important to the future well-being of her children, or the father for whom schooling was always a negative experience may be unable or unwilling to provide the kind of support that contributes to higher levels of student learning. We cannot simply blame the troubles those students may experience on their home lives. We cannot absolve ourselves of our responsibility to help these students learn at high levels because of the conditions into which they were born. These are the students who need us most. A student who completes the K–12 system will spend more than fifteen thousand hours in the care of educators—ample time to impact his or her knowledge, skills, and dispositions in a positive way. It is our responsibility to create the conditions that lead to student success and support and nurture our students as we would want our own children to be nurtured.

Does everyone have to agree on the school's mission?

It is certainly preferable that all members of a staff endorse the premise that the fundamental mission of the school is to ensure high levels of learning (at grade level or better) for all students. Beware, however, of stipulating that everyone must agree before the school can move forward. Any organization that gives each of its members veto power before taking action is certain to experience frustration, delay, and stagnation. You can strive for unanimity, but you must be prepared to settle for consensus.

What is consensus?

Consensus is achieved when (1) all points of view have been not only heard but also solicited and (2) the will of the group is evident, even to those who most oppose it.

What is school culture?

The culture of a school is found in the assumptions, beliefs, expectations, and habits that constitute the norm for the people within that school. The culture of a school can be based on teacher collaboration or isolation; it can be student centered or teacher centered, be based on high expectations or low expectations, involve a growth mindset or a fixed mindset, or embody collective self-efficacy or fatalism. The culture is typically unexamined and simply reflects "the way we do things around here." Reculturing requires bringing unexamined attitudes, beliefs, and habits to the surface for analysis and discussion. The culture of a PLC is always simultaneously loose and tight. (See page 7 for more information.)

What does a school's mission have to do with school culture?

If culture is found in the assumptions, beliefs, and expectations that represent the norm of a school, then a learning-focused school must embrace and commit to the following assumptions.

"We recognize that the fundamental purpose of our school and the reason we come to work each day is to ensure all students learn at high levels. We understand that helping all students learn requires a collective, collaborative effort rather than a series of isolated efforts. Therefore, we work in teams and constantly gather evidence of student learning for two purposes: to inform and improve our individual and collective practice and to better meet the needs of individual students for intervention or extension."

There are two extremely important words in that assumption statement—*ensure* and *all*. The members of a PLC accept collective responsibility to ensure that all students learn at high levels. While factors outside of school impact student learning, the educators understand that they have both the responsibility and ability to ensure that every student masters the academic skills, knowledge, and behaviors needed to succeed in the next year and beyond. Equally important, the educators will assume all students are capable of learning at high levels. The educators reject the temptation to judge a student's academic potential by his or her demographic conditions, such as family economic status, ethnicity, gender, first language, or inclusion in special education. Instead, the school would assume that all students could succeed when they receive targeted, effective instruction at school.

In the end, you have a choice: to be content with the current culture of your school or to consciously and deliberately create your desired culture. If a school cannot build consensus around the fundamental assumptions of a PLC, then the school's culture is misaligned for that aim.

If our school does not have a learning-focused mission and culture, what do we do to change that?

Cultural change is not easy, but it is essential to becoming a PLC. We recommend the following strategies based on the work of Anthony Muhammad (2009).

- **Build an effective school leadership team:** One person cannot transform a school's culture or dictate a school's mission. We recommend that schools create a guiding coalition to lead the change process. This guiding coalition is not the school "dictatorship committee" but a team that learns deeply about best practices, assesses candidly the school's current reality, determines potential next steps to improve the school, identifies possible obstacles and points of leverage, and plans the best way to create staff consensus and ownership. In the end, if a school cannot get even a small group of people to agree on a common direction, it is unlikely that group will be able to convince the entire school.

- **Learn together:** People tend to come to the same conclusions when they base their decisions on the same facts. In a learning community, members arrive at consensus on vital questions by building shared knowledge instead of averaging opinions.

- **Provide the *why* before the *what*:** Too often, leaders introduce change initiatives by describing what needs to be done, without first providing a compelling reason why the change is necessary. In our experience, raising state test scores and staying out of program improvement do not provide a compelling rationale to teachers. Muhammad (2009) recommends using data to create a catalyst for change in an inspirational way, and we have found that many successful schools don't look solely at data such as the percentage of students below proficient on state assessments or the number of kids reading below grade level. Instead, these schools connect these data to individual students—in other words, instead of telling teachers that 12 percent of the school's students are below proficient in reading, they connect those numbers with a list of the specific learners who make up the 12 percent. These connections resonate with our reason for joining the profession—to help kids.

- **Create a doable plan:** The most compelling reason for change will be irrelevant if the staff views the goal as impossible. It is critical that staff members receive a doable plan that defines specifically what leaders will ask of them to achieve this mission and how time and resources will be provided to ensure success.

In our experience, a vast majority of educators enter the profession with a strong desire to help students. If they receive evidence that a learning-focused mission is possible, the realistic steps for how to get there, and the resources and time needed to succeed, most will embrace a learning-focused mission.

What is a guiding coalition?

A guiding coalition is an alliance of key members of an organization who are specifically charged with leading a change process through predictable turmoil. Members of the coalition should include opinion leaders—people who are so respected within the organization that others are likely to follow their lead. Members of the guiding coalition should have shared objectives and high levels of trust. Other terms to describe the guiding coalition include *leadership team, dispersed leadership*, and *getting the right people on the bus*. The underlying premise, however, remains that school and district leaders must have allies if they are going to pursue substantive change. One of the first questions a leader should ask in considering the challenge of such change is, "Who is our guiding coalition?" The guiding coalition could include individual members of existing structures in the school, such as members of a school improvement committee, department chairpeople, or representatives of the teachers association, parental community, and student body. Alternatively, leaders could convene a new structure, such as a task force, for the specific purpose of leading the improvement process.

What happens after we agree to a new learning-focused mission statement?

Once a school community has agreed to a learning-focused mission statement, the members of that community begin the never-ending process of examining and aligning every practice, policy, and procedure within the organization to the mission of learning for all. Collaborative teams within the PLC, as well as the entire staff, will engage in the process of learning together both about the current reality of practices and conditions in their organization and about best practices regarding teaching and learning.

Vision

What is a vision statement, and how does it differ from a mission statement?

Whereas a mission statement answers the question, Why do we exist? a vision statement addresses the question, What do we hope to become? In pursuing the answer to this question, staff members attempt to articulate a compelling, attractive, realistic future that describes what they hope their school will become within the next four or five years.

Why is a vision statement important to being a PLC?

Articulating a shared vision statement provides a sense of direction and a basis for assessing both the current reality of the school and potential strategies, programs, and procedures to improve on that reality.

How long and detailed should a vision statement be?

We've seen vision statements consisting of a few sentences that capture the big ideas of a PLC, and we've seen vision statements that expand on those big ideas, taking up several pages. The length of the statement is not nearly as important as ensuring the statement is shared and it captures the staff's hopes and dreams for the future.

How do we begin the process of writing a vision statement?

The first step in writing a shared vision statement is to identify a guiding coalition of interested stakeholders to lead the process. The formal leader or leaders of the organization will benefit from working through the process with a small group of key staff members and securing them as allies before engaging the entire faculty in the process. Regardless of the structure chosen to represent the guiding coalition, this group of champions for change should engage in building shared knowledge about both the current reality of the organization and best practices regarding improvement. After building shared knowledge, the guiding coalition should create a draft of the vision statement to share with and solicit input from all the stakeholders throughout the organization.

Who should be involved in writing the vision statement?

Initially, the members of the guiding coalition (see the answer to the previous question) should take the lead in creating a draft of the vision statement. After sharing the draft with all stakeholders of the organization, members of the guiding coalition should meet with the stakeholders in small groups to solicit feedback, clarify ideas, make revisions, and ultimately build consensus on the statement until it represents the shared vision of the members of the organization.

Does everyone have to agree on the school's vision?

The impact of a vision statement will depend, to a large extent, on the degree to which it connects to the hopes, dreams, and aspirations of the school's staff. Establishing such a vision requires a consensus-building process that relies much more on conversations than presentations, and on dialogue more than monologue. Once again, however, there is a difference between consensus and unanimity. (See the response under "Does everyone have to agree on the school's mission?" on page 18.) Consensus requires that (1) all points of view have been not only heard but also solicited and (2) the will of the group is evident, even to those who most oppose it. Note that this definition of *consensus* does not require universal approval, nor does it allow for an individual or handful of people to exercise veto power over the will of the group. So though not everyone is required to endorse the vision, it must represent what is clearly the will of the group. Leaders must expect those who have reservations to act in accordance with the vision.

What happens after we have agreed on a new learning-focused vision statement?

The process of writing a shared vision statement will impact the school only if leaders take purposeful steps to demonstrate that actually becoming the school in the vision is the collective responsibility of every member of the staff. Whether an organization realizes its shared vision will depend far less on what is written or said (the verbiage) and much more on what is done (the actions).

Members of a PLC must align their actions to the shared vision and mission. The third pillar of the shared foundation, values or collective commitments, addresses the need for schools and districts to translate the aspirations in the vision statement into actions that will lead to the attainment of the vision.

▮ Values

What are values?

In a PLC, values are the collective commitments educators must establish regarding the specific attitudes and behaviors they will demonstrate in order to advance the organization's vision. Articulated values answer the question, How must we behave in order to make our shared vision a reality?

What are collective commitments?

Collective commitments and values are synonymous in the shared foundation of a PLC. As stated in the previous answer, collective commitments are the specific attitudes and behaviors people within the organization pledge to demonstrate in order to advance their shared vision. Collective commitments answer the question, How must we behave—today and every day—in order to make our shared vision a reality?

Collective commitments guide the individual work of each member of the staff and outline how each person can contribute to the shared mission and vision of the organization. When members of an organization understand the purpose of their organization, know where it is headed, and then pledge to act in certain ways to move it in the right direction, they don't need prescriptive rules and regulations to guide their daily work. Policy manuals and directives are replaced by commitments and covenants.

Are collective commitments the same as team norms?

In PLCs, team norms represent commitments developed by each team to guide its members in working together. Norms help team members clarify expectations regarding how they will work together to achieve their shared goals. In that sense, team norms represent the collective commitments team members make to one another.

Schoolwide collective commitments, the third pillar of the shared foundation of a PLC, capture the broad, tight behaviors that each member of the faculty and staff must honor. Examples of these include the following.

- We commit to be positive, contributing members of our collaborative teams.
- We commit to teach the agreed-on guaranteed curriculum.
- We commit to develop and administer common formative assessments to monitor student learning on an ongoing basis.

- We commit to use the evidence of student learning from our common assessments to address the learning needs of each student entrusted to us.

- We commit to use the evidence of student learning from our common assessments to inform and improve our professional practice.

Team norms address more specific behaviors that make for effective collaboration. Examples of these include the following.

- We commit to begin and end our meetings on time.

- We commit to be fully engaged in and contribute to the work of our collaborative team.

- We commit to be respectful listeners during team discussions.

Goals

What are goals in a PLC?

Goals are measurable milestones that leaders can use to assess progress in advancing toward a vision. Whereas the mission pillar asks, "Why do we exist?"; the vision pillar asks, "What must we become?"; and the values pillar asks, "How must we behave?" the goals pillar asks, "What results do we seek, and how will we know we are making progress?" Goals represent targets and timelines.

How do goals relate to a school's mission and vision?

Because the mission of a PLC school or district is to ensure high levels of learning for all, goals in a PLC include learning-focused improvement targets. Achieving an improvement target means more students or staff members have learned at higher levels. The goal-setting process requires educators to:

- Establish learning-focused goals

- Learn together about new and different ways to achieve those goals

- Put the new learning into action

- Gather evidence of learning

- Celebrate when goals are achieved

- Establish new learning-focused goals

How do we start the goal-writing process?

The goal-writing process begins with members of a team, school faculty, or district community gathering and examining evidence of their current reality. As they learn together about trends in student learning, they identify and celebrate areas of improvement, and they also identify an area or two in greatest need of improvement in which to establish their goals.

What kind of information should a team collect to determine their current reality?

Team members should collect and examine multiple indicators of student learning and other factors that have an impact on whether students are learning. In effect, every school and every team within a school should "paint a data picture" of its current reality. Visit the AllThingsPLC website for a template that can be of assistance with the process of painting a picture of your current reality (www.allthingsplc.info /files/uploads/adatapictureofourschool.pdf).

What is a SMART goal?

If a team, by definition, is a group of people working interdependently to achieve a common goal for which each member is mutually accountable, then setting goals is essential to the collaborative team process. And because a results orientation—the third big idea—is such an important aspect of the PLC process, the SMART goal acronym offers a terrific tool that helps shift a team's focus from activity to results. A SMART goal is (Conzemius & O'Neill, 2006):

- **S**trategic and specific
- **M**easurable
- **A**ttainable
- **R**esults oriented
- **T**ime bound

Collaborative teams in PLC schools and districts pursue SMART goals to help them monitor and celebrate incremental improvement toward achieving the vision and mission of the organization.

Setting a SMART goal is a relatively simple process in a school committed to continuous improvement. Imagine a school that establishes a schoolwide goal to improve student achievement in every subject and grade level. Each team within the school will be asked to address all points on the acronym as it establishes a team SMART goal.

What is strategic in relation to a SMART goal?

A strategic team goal is one that is aligned to the bigger, broader goals of the organization. When a team achieves a strategic goal, members experience improvement for their team and the students entrusted to them, and they also contribute to improving student achievement in the entire organization.

What is measurable in relation to a SMART goal?

In order to establish a measurable goal, each team should receive data that help members establish the current reality regarding student achievement in their subject and grade level. Once the team is clear on the current reality, it then establishes a measurable improvement target that represents higher student achievement than the current reality.

What is attainable in relation to a SMART goal?

Leaders encourage members of each team to set their improvement target at a level the members consider attainable—the team members believe they can achieve the target if they work interdependently.

What is results oriented in relation to a SMART goal?

Team members must identify the evidence of student learning (results) they will monitor throughout the year and at the end of the year to determine whether more students are learning at higher levels. Results—evidence of student learning—may come from multiple data points, including common assessments (assessments administered to all students in that course or grade-level subject). When a team attains a results-oriented goal, then more students will have learned at higher levels than in the past.

What is time bound in relation to a SMART goal?

Time bound means that team members identify on their pacing guide or curriculum map when they will gather evidence of student learning, including a target date when members will examine final results to indicate whether the team has achieved its goal.

What is the difference between a learning goal and a teaching goal?

A learning goal focuses on outcomes—improving student (learning) results. A teaching goal focuses on inputs—the activities or actions the teacher will use during instruction. In the PLC process, teams pursue SMART goals, which, by the very nature of addressing all points of the acronym, are learning focused. We refer to the teacher inputs as strategies or action steps rather than goals.

Who writes the goals in a PLC—the district, school, or team?

Teams at each level should write their own goals, but the goals at each level, although different, must align toward one common goal. We acknowledge that the grain size of goals will be different from level to level, but in a PLC, the district, school, and grade- or course-level teams all write goals that are interdependent, linked to one another, and focused on the same outcome.

Fragmented or unaligned goals only serve to waste energy, waste resources, and generate cynicism. Likewise, the practice of flitting from one hot topic to the next rarely results in sustained improvement. To ensure success, goals at all levels should be limited in number and focused on the right work. We strongly recommend that districts, schools, and grade- or course-level teams limit the number of goals to a few multiyear goals that directly link to the big ideas of a PLC. Leaders should not add a goal, initiative, or project to the list of goals at the district, school, or team level until and unless there is a strong argument for how it will promote the basic tenets of a PLC.

Do site goals need to align to district goals?

Yes. When a district establishes goals that focus on improving student achievement —and hopes to achieve them—then site goals must align to district goals. If schools are allowed to reject district goals or pursue their own unrelated goals, there is no strategic alignment between the two entities.

Do team goals need to align to site goals?

Yes. When a school establishes goals that focus on improving student achievement —and hopes to achieve them—then team goals must align to school goals. Once leaders establish a goal at any level of the organization, they must call on the people who are crucial to achieving it to contribute to doing so.

How many goals should a team have?

The research has not identified a specific number of goals that will maximize success, but experience has shown that the adage "less is more" holds true for goals. More progress is typically generated by fewer goals. It is hard to imagine any team being able to focus on more than three or four goals during the course of a single school year. More important than the number of goals is their focus—it must be on the right work. We devote chapter 4 of *Learning by Doing, Third Edition* (DuFour et al., 2016), to writing effective, results-oriented SMART goals.

Should goals address short-term outcomes or long-term achievements?

In the PLC process, teams, schools, and districts establish both short- and long-term goals. Short-term SMART goals are intended to document incremental progress and build momentum and self-efficacy through short-term wins. Long-term stretch goals will require deep, significant changes throughout the organization to achieve. Stretch goals are intended to inspire, to capture the imagination of people within the organization, to stimulate creativity and innovation, and to serve as a unifying focal point of effort.

Should the team also create an action plan for each goal?

Teams must create action plans that include not only the goals of the team and larger organization but also the strategies the team will implement, responsibilities of each team member, and timelines for gathering evidence of student learning. Examples of team action plans and a SMART goal template are available in chapter 4 of *Learning by Doing, Third Edition* (DuFour et al., 2016). (Visit **go.SolutionTree .com/PLCbooks** to download free reproducibles.)

How can a team monitor progress on end-of-year goals?

See if this scenario sounds familiar: a team writes a SMART goal and turns it in to the principal, who dutifully checks it off the list and files it away on the shelf. Using this kind of "share and shelve" approach to goal setting dramatically reduces the likelihood of meaningful progress on the goal. Goals have little effect on improving teaching and learning unless leaders monitor and measure progress toward the goal on an ongoing basis.

The most effective way to monitor progress on end-of-year goals is to turn them into during-the-year goals and monitor them on a routine basis throughout the school year. Too many times, districts, schools, or teams write SMART goals but fail to look at them again until the end of the year. At that point, it's too late to do anything about them.

A good time to check on progress toward a goal is right after a team reviews the results of a common assessment. Teams in Kildeer Countryside Community Consolidated School District 96 followed a simple process to create a short-term SMART goal for each unit that was linked to their yearlong SMART goal. The short-term SMART goal created milestones along the way to measure and monitor progress toward the goal.

Where can we find examples of effective mission statements, vision statements, collective commitments, and goals that are serving as a solid foundation of the PLC process?

Adlai E. Stevenson High School District 125 in Lincolnshire, Illinois, has established a solid foundation for a PLC by addressing the mission, vision, collective commitments, and goals of the district. To view the vision statement (which has been adopted as board policy), visit the district website (www.d125.org/about /school-board/district-125-board-of-education-vision-statement).

The district has taken steps to translate the vision into collective commitments from various stakeholders. Visit the following webpages to view those commitments from each stakeholder group.

- **Board and admin team:** www.d125.org/about/vision/collective -commitments-board-and-admin-team
- **Faculty:** www.d125.org/about/vision/collective-commitments-faculty
- **Support staff:** www.d125.org/about/vision/collective-commitments -support-staff
- **Students:** www.d125.org/about/vision/collective-commitments-students
- **Parents:** www.d125.org/about/vision/collective-commitments-parents

Schaumburg District 54 in suburban Chicago offers an excellent example of districtwide mission, vision, commitments, and goals. Visit Community Consolidated School District 54's website to see this example (http://sd54.org/board/files/2010/04/Mission-Vision -Commitments-and-Goals-English-7-1-151.pdf).

Mason Crest Elementary School in Fairfax County, Virginia, also provides an excellent example of a shared foundation for a single school. Visit Mason Crest's website to see this example of a shared foundation (www.fcps.edu/masoncrestes/about /missionVision.html).

Where can we find examples of SMART goals from highly effective teams in PLC schools?

Examples of team SMART goals are available in chapter 4 of *Learning by Doing, Third Edition* (DuFour et al., 2016). Visit **go.SolutionTree.com/PLCbooks** to download free reproducibles.

What other resources can we study to learn more about SMART goals?

Chapter 4 of *Learning by Doing, Third Edition* (DuFour et al., 2016), includes additional information and resources regarding SMART goals. There are also multiple blog articles posted on AllThingsPLC (www.allthingsplc.info) about goal setting. We recommend the following blog posts.

- *Team SMART Goals vs. Smart Students* by Rick DuFour and Becky DuFour: www.allthingsplc.info/blog/view/24/team-smart-goals-vs-smart-students

- *What Is the Sequence of Goal Setting in a PLC?* by Rick DuFour and Becky DuFour: www.allthingsplc.info/blog/view/57/what-is-the-sequence-of-goal-setting-in-a-plc

- *Moving School Improvement Into the Classroom With SMART Goals* by Dennis King: www.allthingsplc.info/blog/view/159/moving-school-improvement-into-the-classroom-with-smart-goals

- *Realistic SMART Goals* by Rick DuFour: www.allthingsplc.info/blog/view/244/realistic-smart-goals

A Solid Foundation

How long should it take to create and build consensus on mission, vision, values, and goals?

We have seen an entire faculty complete building consensus for mission, vision, values, and goals by devoting two full days to that process at the start of the school year before students arrived. This concentrated block of time is an excellent way to establish a solid foundation. We have seen a guiding coalition do the preliminary work of building shared knowledge of the current reality and most promising practices for school improvement with the entire staff once the school year started. Representatives of the coalition then met with the faculty in small groups to address questions and concerns. Finally, the coalition met once again with small groups to determine if the staff supported the proposals for mission, vision, values, and goals (see "What is consensus?," page 19). This process took about two months to complete.

Our advice is to push forward with building shared knowledge and consensus as quickly as possible. The real test of your foundation will not be its eloquence but rather will be the degree to which your staff understands and supports it and the extent to which you use it to guide the day-to-day decisions and procedures of the school. The longer it takes to create the shared foundation, the longer your school will operate without its benefits.

Should the foundation of mission, vision, values, and goals be established at the school level or the district level?

Both. It is entirely appropriate for a district to establish the conditions it hopes to create in every school. Ownership of decisions, however, is directly related to the level of engagement people are afforded in making those decisions. A districtwide foundation typically includes *representative groups* of teachers, administrators, parents, and other stakeholders. A school's foundation, on the other hand, provides an opportunity to include *every* staff member in the process. Of course, a school's mission, vision, values, and goals should be consistent with and supportive of the district's shared foundation; but school staff benefit from greater clarity and commitment when they engage in the process at the school level.

How often should a district or school revise its mission and vision?

The mission of a district or school—ensuring high levels of learning for all—should remain constant over time. The vision of what it takes to create such a school may change from time to time. We strongly recommend, however, that the vision should remain in place for at least five years before reconsidering it. It takes some time to make progress toward a shared vision. Furthermore, a constantly moving target discourages educators from trying to achieve it.

What happens if a school skips creating the foundation?

When educators lack a clear sense of purpose, a shared vision of what they are attempting to create, the necessary commitments to move the school in the desired direction, and goals to serve as targets and timelines for their process, it is impossible to engage in the collaborative, collective effort that is essential to improving student learning. As a result, individual educators work in isolation as disconnected islands of autonomy, and students are subjected to an educational lottery in which what they learn depends exclusively on the individual teacher to whom they have been assigned rather than on the school they attend. In short, without a shared foundation to shape a new culture and structure for schooling, schools will continue to operate as they have for more than a century, with decidedly unequal learning and opportunities for the students they serve.

Are we a PLC if we read and discuss the same professional books and articles?

No. Reading and discussing the same books and articles are ways for staff to build shared knowledge or learn together, but that is only one aspect of the PLC process. When members of PLCs are called on to resolve an issue or make a decision, they consistently attempt to learn together by clarifying questions and accessing the same information and knowledge base. But they don't stop there. Members of PLCs understand that the most powerful learning always occurs in a context of taking action, and they value engagement and experience as the most effective teachers.

Is there a difference between small learning communities and professional learning communities?

Yes. The small learning community (SLC) movement was based on the premise that if schools (particularly high schools) were smaller, teachers and students could establish more positive relationships, leading to higher levels of student achievement. The Gates Foundation helped fund the movement and hired two independent research firms to assess its impact—the American Institutes for Research and SRI International (2005, 2006). The researchers issued the following findings in their reports.

- The attendance rate of students in the restructured SLCs was worse than attendance in other schools in the district.

- When taking previous achievement into account, students showed slightly better performance in language arts but worse performance in mathematics than other high school students in the same district.

- The quality of student work was low in the restructured schools.

- Demanding and unwieldy teacher workloads "may be endemic to the staffing structures of many small high schools" (American Institutes for Research & SRI International, 2005, p. 4), and the resulting teacher burnout threatened the viability of the initiative. The structure resulted in most teachers operating as singletons without the benefit of a collaborative teaching team. Staff turnover at these schools was high.

Both research groups reported that the SLC had not altered the entrenched culture of educators and their assumptions regarding student achievement. The reports recommended that the Gates Foundation "rethink the school redesign strategy" (American Institutes for Research & SRI International, 2006, p. 82). Furthermore, the reports state:

> Although there have been some isolated examples of apparently successful small schools emerging from the restructuring of a large high school, these have been the exception rather than the rule. On the whole, the data that we have for school redesign efforts are not encouraging. (American Institutes for Research & SRI International, 2006, p. 82)

A better hope for changing schools is to emphasize continuous monitoring of student learning, a tight school culture, and greater attention to issues of curriculum and instruction.

The PLC process does not concern itself with the size of the school and instead focuses on what the SLC movement did not: establishing a culture that is simultaneously loose and tight, clarifying the intended learning outcomes for every student, monitoring each student's learning on an ongoing basis, using the evidence of student learning to inform and improve individual and collective professional practice, and creating systems of intervention and enrichment to better meet the needs of individual students. PLCs have been highly effective both in very small schools and in schools with more than four thousand students.

Additional PLC Resources to Dig Deeper: Mission, Vision, Values, and Goals

- DuFour, R., DuFour, R., & Eaker, R. (2008). *Revisiting Professional Learning Communities at Work: New insights for improving schools.* Bloomington, IN: Solution Tree Press.

- DuFour, R., DuFour, R., Eaker, R., Many, T. W., & Mattos, M. (2016). *Learning by doing: A handbook for Professional Learning Communities at Work* (3rd ed.). Bloomington, IN: Solution Tree Press.

Final Thoughts

Educators are tempted to rush into the work of a PLC without first establishing a shared foundation. They want teachers assigned to teams, time provided for collaboration, essential standards identified, common exams written, and systems of intervention established. But without the benefit of shared mission, vision, values, and goals, these activities represent discrete tasks rather than a comprehensive, collective effort to create a new kind of school.

As we stated in the introduction, no competent builder would consider building a structure without a solid foundation. That foundation may be less visible than some of the other tasks of construction, but it is vital to the quality of the finished product. The same is true in building the foundation of a PLC. When done well, it provides the purpose and direction for the collective efforts that follow. Don't skip establishing a solid foundation of shared mission, vision, values, and goals.

Chapter 2

Fostering a Collaborative Culture

The single biggest obstacle educators must overcome if they are to transform their schools into PLCs is the long-standing tradition of teachers working in isolation. The assumption that the fundamental structure of the school is the isolated classroom in which a single teacher is responsible for his or her students must give way to a new model in which the collaborative team of teachers serves as the core structure and the engine that drives the school improvement process. Team members work interdependently to achieve common goals for which they are mutually accountable. The team is part of a collective process to promote both student and adult learning.

In order to move from a culture of isolation to a culture of collaboration, teachers must be:

- Assigned into meaningful rather than artificial teams

- Provided with time to collaborate on a regular basis

- Absolutely clear on the nature of the work they must do

- Furnished with oversight, resources, and support to ensure they can succeed at what they are being asked to do

The most common mistakes schools make when attempting to create a collaborative culture include the following.

- They invite or encourage educators to collaborate rather than embedding required collaboration in the routine practice of the school.

- They allow educators to function as groups rather than teams.

- They fail to focus on the right work.

In this chapter, we will answer the questions most frequently asked when a school or district creates a collaborative culture.

Forming Teams

What is the difference between a PLC and a team, committee, or task force?

The PLC is the larger organization (the school or the district). Members of the PLC engage in a recurring cycle of collective inquiry and action research in order to achieve better results for the students they serve.

The collaborative team is made up of educators who share students or content and who work interdependently to achieve common SMART goals for which members are mutually accountable.

A common mistake is to refer to a collaborative team as a PLC. It is not. There are elements of the PLC process that leaders must address on a schoolwide basis that are beyond the scope of a team. Thus, the larger organization (school or district) is the PLC, and it is composed of collaborative teams.

A committee is typically a standing body with responsibility for a particular aspect of the school—for example, the discipline committee, the textbook committee, the technology committee, and so on. Committees typically continue to function from year to year.

A task force is typically a temporary group that focuses on a single issue or task. Leaders charge members with investigating options and build shared knowledge on the issue in question, develop recommendations, and help build consensus for their proposals. The task force generally disbands when it completes its work.

In summary, the district or school serves as the PLC with collaborative teams serving as the fundamental structure of the PLC. Collaborative teams are essential to the PLC process. The school may also use the committee and task force structures, and while they may serve useful purposes, they are not essential to the PLC process.

What criteria should we use when forming collaborative teacher teams?

Collaboration alone will not guarantee your school will get better results. Collaboration is only powerful when teams focus on the right work. Teacher team collaboration in the PLC process is guided by four critical questions.

1. What is it we want our students to learn? What knowledge, skills, and dispositions do we expect them to acquire?

2. How will we know our students are learning? What evidence will we gather to ensure students understand the skills and concepts we are teaching?

3. How will we respond when some of our students don't learn?

4. How will we respond when many of our students have already demonstrated proficiency in the skill or concept under consideration?

Answering these questions effectively requires team members to share essential curriculum. So the criterion for forming teams is to base assignments on which team members have a shared responsibility for answering these questions together.

Is there an optimum size for a teacher team?

Researchers have been unable to arrive at a consensus regarding the optimum size of a team. There have been powerful teams of two—the Wright Brothers, Lennon and McCartney, and Brin and Page (the creators of Google). Large teams have also accomplished great things. Steve Jobs created a team of fifty people to develop the Macintosh computer. The Manhattan Project, which oversaw the creation of the atomic bomb, was the largest collaboration of scientists in the history of the United States up to that time. More than 150,000 engineers, contractors, military personnel, and construction workers contributed to the project. In her book *Team Moon*, Catherine Thimmesh (2006) refers to the 400,000 people who worked on the Apollo 11 project as "the greatest team ever."

It would, therefore, be completely arbitrary to attempt to declare the definitive optimum size for the collaborative teams within a PLC. It also would be foolish for eight teachers assigned to teach sophomore English to exclude one member from participating on the team because members had decided that seven was the optimum number.

The size of the team certainly impacts the way it operates. A team of twenty-five members will function differently from one with four or five members. The larger team will likely divide tasks among smaller subgroups, convene more frequently in subgroups, and reserve larger team meetings for reviewing recommendations and making decisions.

Can a team be too small or too big?

A team can be effective with as few as two members and as many as a virtually unlimited number of members; size will, however, impact how the team operates. The more important questions are, Do these teachers have shared responsibility for student learning? and Will they be asked to work interdependently to achieve common goals for which members are mutually accountable?

How many teams should a teacher be on?

Because teachers are asked to contribute to the success of the team, we recommend they serve on no more than two teams. For example, an elementary special education teacher might serve on the special education team and one grade-level team where the special education caseload is the largest. A high school social studies teacher might be assigned to the world history team and the U.S. history team. If that teacher is teaching more than two courses, leaders should allow him or her to select the two teams to contribute to but also expect him or her to honor the decisions made by the third team.

What is the best format for elementary teacher teams?

Researchers consistently recommend that the best team structure in an elementary school is the grade-level team (Saphier, King, & D'Auria, 2006; Saunders, Goldenberg, & Gallimore, 2009; Wei, Darling-Hammond, Andree, Richardson, & Orphanos, 2009). This team structure is ideally suited to the collective inquiry into the four critical questions of a PLC.

1. What do students need to know and be able to do?

2. How will we know when they have learned it?

3. What will we do when they haven't learned it?

4. What will we do when they already know it?

In addition to including all teachers from the same grade level on the same team, the school should also look for "logical links" so that instructional resource and support teachers can contribute to the work of grade-level teams. Very often, however, resource teachers and specialists serve students in multiple grade levels and courses, and therefore, leaders cannot expect them to contribute to every team. We recommend that these teachers select one or two teams each year to co-labor with on a regular basis and build schedules to accommodate their participation. For example, the special education resource teacher may have more designated students in second and fifth grades than any other grades this year; therefore, the special education teacher joins those two grade-level teams. A reading specialist could join kindergarten and first-grade teams to work with both the teachers and students in building a strong literacy foundation. An English language teacher could join a third-grade team to support the large number of English learners at that grade level. In these examples, the resource teachers have mutual accountability with the other team members for the learning success of designated students assigned to those grade levels.

What if, at our elementary school, each grade level has subject-specific teachers? How do we team?

If, by departmentalizing across a grade level, one teacher is solely responsible for every student at the grade level learning mathematics, while another is solely responsible for English language arts, another for science, and another for social studies, then the structure does not support the definition of *team* in the PLC process: a group of people working *interdependently* to achieve a *common goal* for which members are *mutually accountable*. In effect, this arrangement creates four singleton teachers who are more likely to function as an interdisciplinary *group* rather than a collaborative *team*. Research on interdisciplinary teams versus content teams consistently concludes that the content team structure leads to higher levels of student learning than interdisciplinary or departmentalized teams (Saphier et al., 2006; Saunders et al., 2009; Wei et al., 2009).

Given that research connects content- or subject-specific teams to higher levels of learning—and given that the core curriculum in the upper elementary grades is vast and deeply packed—some schools are creating effective subteams within a grade level, allowing two or more teachers to take responsibility for the same subject.

In the earlier example of the four-member team, rather than each teacher specializing in one subject area, the team agrees that every teacher will teach both English language arts and mathematics because the stakes for elementary students are so high if they are not successful in these significant content areas. Each teacher at the grade level commits to be *mutually accountable* for student learning in those two subjects. The team then departmentalizes for the other subjects (for example, two teachers partner for science, while the other two partner for social studies).

A six-member grade-level team shared a slightly different approach. Every teacher agreed to teach English language arts. The team established a shared goal for improving student learning in English language arts. The members worked interdependently and supported one another as they planned and delivered first best instruction in each classroom, and they created team-developed common formative assessments for English language arts and administered them to all students in the grade level. The team analyzed the results and provided systematic intervention and enrichment for all the students. In addition, the team subdivided responsibility for the other content areas: two teachers took responsibility for student learning in mathematics, two in science, and two in social studies.

Fostering Collaboration

How do we form teams at a small elementary school with only one teacher per grade level?

A small elementary school with only one teacher per grade level could structure itself into vertical teams—for example, a K–1 team, a grades 2–3 team, and a grades 4–5 team. In this example, the three vertical teams would address the four critical questions of a PLC for both grades (subject by subject over time) and would take collective responsibility to support each other and help each other's students learn at high levels. The school could enhance the vertical teams with any other instructional support staff members who are available. For example, the speech and language pathologist joins the K–1 team, the special education teacher joins the grades 2–3 team, and the librarian joins the grades 4–5 team.

In addition to creating vertical teams within the building, each teacher may also benefit from joining a job-alike electronic team. Although vertical structures may provide a collaborative team for the singletons within a school, they do not provide grade-level or same-course collaboration. Electronic teams can address that void. Educators seeking teammates beyond their school campuses can turn to their district office, regional service center, or professional organizations to find job-alike partners. Members of electronic teams use the available technology to support their collaborative process.

We have combination teachers at our elementary school. What team should they be on?

The vertical structure described in the previous answer is often useful in PLC schools where students sit in multigrade or combination classrooms. For example, the grades 2 and 3 combination teacher collaborates with the other second- *and* third-grade teachers on the grades 2–3 vertical team. Some larger elementary schools with multiple teachers at each grade level—and a few combination classrooms—have both straight grade-level teams and vertical teams to ensure the combination teachers collaborate with teachers who teach the exact same content as they do.

Who should elementary specialist teachers like art, music, and physical education teachers team with?

Although there is no one right answer to this important question, several options follow for specialist teachers who are singletons in their schools to be members of a high-performing collaborative team.

- **District or regional teams:** Teachers who are singletons in their schools can become members of district or regional job-alike teams. They can meet in face-to-face settings periodically, but most often, the team agrees on a common block of weekly time for collaboration so that members can remain in their school settings and use technology to facilitate collaboration.

- **Logical links teams:** Resource teachers, support teachers, and specialists can join grade-level teams that are pursuing outcomes linked to their areas of expertise. We recommend that these teachers select one or two teams each year to co-labor with on a regular basis and to build schedules to accommodate their participation. They often make these team selections based on a large number of students in a particular grade level needing extra support. Other times, specialists may select a team because they would like to become more familiar with the content or because they feel they have particular expertise they could contribute to the team.

- **Vertical teams:** Specialists can join vertical teams with their job-alike colleagues in the district. If the proximity of the schools does not allow for face-to-face meetings, team members use available technology to facilitate electronic collaboration. For example, a band teacher at the middle school has a vested interest in working with the elementary band teacher so that they can create a great band program. If the principals of the two schools could coordinate the teachers' schedules for a collaborative meeting once each week, the band teachers could meet electronically to agree on skills, content, and performance standards students should achieve at their various grade levels and how to assess whether their students are achieving the standards. They could record performances or rehearsals to share with their teammates, jointly assess the strengths and weaknesses of the performance, and discuss ways to improve upon it. They could set SMART goals regarding the ratings their bands get in competitions or the number of students who qualify for distinction in the regional or state band or the number of students who remain in band from fifth to sixth grade.

These vertical teams should have the same expectations as teachers of the core curriculum at each grade level. Teachers agree on what they want students to learn, the standard of quality they seek, and the criteria they will use in assessing the quality of student work. They practice applying the criteria until they can assess the same work consistently (inter-rater reliability), and then they use the results (the evidence of student learning) to consider ways they can improve student performance. They set SMART goals each year to help more students achieve at higher levels and establish norms about how they will work together.

Fostering Collaboration

We recommend that resource and specialist teachers participate in the decision regarding their team assignment. Over time, these teachers can rotate team membership from year to year as adult and student learning needs change.

Who should a dual-immersion teacher team with when the other grade-level teachers are English only?

Even though the language may be different, the concepts and skills students are expected to know and be able to do are the same. Therefore, one vitally important team structure to include is logical links (described in the previous answer). A third-grade dual-immersion teacher, for example, becomes a member of the third-grade team. Some additional team structure options may also be beneficial.

- **District or regional teams:** The third-grade dual-immersion teacher in one school can become a member of a district or regional job-alike team. The team can meet in face-to-face settings periodically, but most often, the team agrees on a common block of weekly time for collaboration so that members can remain in their school settings and use technology to facilitate collaboration.

- **Vertical teams:** The third-grade dual-immersion teachers could team vertically with the second- and fourth-grade dual-immersion teachers. This team could work to ensure that a strong scope and sequence of curriculum, assessment, and learning support occurs every day, year after year, for the students in the dual-immersion program.

On our grade-level team, one teacher is assigned to gifted students, one to regular students, and one to English learners and mainstreamed students. How do we team together with such different student needs?

First and foremost, grouping students by ability (gifted, regular, English learner, and so on) is misaligned with ensuring high levels of learning for all. A meta-analysis of more than three hundred studies on ability grouping (tracking) shows that "tracking has minimal effects on learning outcomes and profound negative equity effects" (Hattie, 2009, p. 90).

The following blog post by Jennifer Deinhart (2015), a K–8 mathematics specialist at Mason Crest Elementary School in Fairfax County, Virginia, provides additional information about the equity issue and some alternative approaches to grouping students that are much more aligned with ensuring high levels of learning for all.

When students are grouped by ability in different classrooms, there are three factors that can have a negative impact.

1. Students in the struggling and middle groups will not have the vocal models and exposure to the rich talk of the higher-achieving students. These models often provide great examples of how to defend thinking around mathematical ideas and share processes and ideas that may connect better with students than the language of the teacher alone.

2. While the intent of structuring classrooms according to ability may be to create a pace that is more manageable for students, more often expectations are lowered and the work is over-scaffolded. Students learn best when there is a balance of struggle and support. It is important that all students are held to high expectations (the end goals are all the same, right?) and that they have opportunities to problem solve through mistakes with guidance such as questioning from the teacher.

3. Make no mistake, students will know what group they are placed in, regardless of how it is communicated or how disguised the levels are. This often leads to the self-fulfilling prophecy that they are not good enough to handle rigorous learning experiences.

So if grouping classrooms in this way can have such a negative impact, here are four ways that we try to meet the various needs of our learners in heterogeneous classrooms.

1. Consider flexibly grouping students for guided instruction that changes based on common formative assessment data from unit tests, performance tasks, and exit tickets. In this way, you will be setting up your guided instruction in your mathematics workshop much like you would in guided reading. Students change as they show mastery of concepts.

2. Alternate grouping in the classroom between homogeneous groups and heterogeneous groups. Students with different levels of ability can often partner to tackle a problem, task, or game.

3. Differentiate techniques such as tiered tasks. These tasks cover the exact same objective but start at a level that is either on grade level or below and gradually increase in number and rigor to the grade-level standard and beyond. Students move through the tasks at their own pace, but since they are so similar, a teacher can manage instruction with a group of students in various places.

4. Create opportunities for spiraling back to objectives when students need extra time and support. This is when looking at the data from your formative assessments can really drive how you structure your mathematics workshop to include both current and review topics.

Fostering Collaboration

I teach early childhood, so whom do I team with?

Like any other grade in school, preK has identified curriculum and learning outcomes designed to prepare students for future success in school, usually from frameworks provided at the state or regional level, or available from national organizations. Early childhood teachers should team with other teachers teaching the same learning outcomes. Most often, a preK program has more than one teacher, so forming a preK team of educators to focus on the four critical questions of a PLC is logical. A second option would be forming a vertical team with the kindergarten teachers whom the preK students will transition to when they begin elementary school. This vertical team makes sense, as many of the skills taught in early childhood programs are essential standards that are also taught in kindergarten.

What is the best format for secondary school teacher teams?

The best structure for secondary school teacher teams is the course-specific structure; that is, all teachers who teach biology would form one team, all teachers who teach U.S. history would be on another, and so on. This team structure, once again, is ideally suited to collective inquiry into the four critical questions of a PLC.

1. What is it we want our students to learn? What knowledge, skills, and dispositions do we expect them to acquire?

2. How will we know our students are learning? What evidence will we gather to ensure students understand the skills and concepts we are teaching?

3. How will we respond when some of our students don't learn?

4. How will we respond when many of our students have already demonstrated proficiency in the skill or concept under consideration?

Interdisciplinary teams can be a viable option, but often members focus on the behavior of individual students rather than on working interdependently to improve learning for all students. If the interdisciplinary team is to be effective in the PLC process, members must pursue a common learning goal for which members are mutually accountable. For example, an interdisciplinary middle school team could commit to help every seventh-grade student learn to write persuasively.

I teach AP U.S. history at our school, while my colleague teaches the regular U.S. history classes. How do we team together?

The key question to ask in establishing a team is, "Do these teachers share the same content or the same students?" In this case, the answer to both is, "They do not."

The AP history course has intended outcomes that are different from a regular high school history course's outcomes. If there is more than one teacher assigned to teach AP history, those teachers should be a team, and likewise, all the regular U.S. history teachers should form a different team. If there is only one teacher assigned to each course, the school has created a structure that supports isolation rather than collaboration. Both teachers should teach some sections of each course, and they could then serve as a team of two to support one another in helping students succeed.

Our middle school has "villages" with grade-level interdisciplinary teams. How do we team?

The four critical questions that drive the work of teacher teams in the PLC process start with the first question: What is it we want our students to learn? Teachers who teach the same subject and course can best answer this curricular question. There are times when approaching this question from an interdisciplinary approach is helpful; however, it is unlikely that an eighth-grade English language arts teacher would gain much benefit determining essential ELA standards by meeting with eighth-grade mathematics, science, social studies, and physical education teachers on a weekly basis. Instead, for that ELA teacher to improve his or her knowledge and skills at identifying, teaching, and assessing eighth-grade ELA standards, it would be much better if he or she met with other eighth-grade ELA teachers.

If an interdisciplinary team—a *village*—is going to form a team within a PLC, the team members must share essential learning outcomes that they will collaborate on to ensure their students master them. The key criterion is the word *essential*. The team should not be reaching for just something in common to collaborate around; members should be collaborating on truly critical skills and knowledge, which the team deems so important to future success in school that every student *must* master them. This creates both value and urgency for the team members' work together. While an interdisciplinary team may not share specific content knowledge across courses, the team could focus on higher-level thinking skills that span the curriculum, such as argumentation or analytical reading.

(For an additional perspective on this question, see chapter 1, "Is there a difference between small learning communities and professional learning communities?" page 33.)

I am a singleton elective teacher. Whom do I team with?

Collaboration is most powerful when teachers can team with educators who do what they do—who share the same "day job." So, if a middle school band teacher wants to get better at teaching middle school band, who would be the best people for him or her to collaborate with? Other middle school band teachers, of course! The same can be said for any elective teacher, such as teachers of art, drama, industrial technology, home economics, business applications, foreign language, video production, yearbook, student government, web design, and graphic arts. While many of these positions are often taught by a single teacher on secondary campuses, almost every school in a specific region or district has similar courses. When this is the case, forming electronic teams between job-alike teachers can be powerful. (See the question, "I have been assigned to an electronic team. How do we team?" on page 51 for ideas on how to team electronically.)

We have also seen examples of elective teachers forming vertical teams across a district. For example, secondary teachers who teach Spanish across a middle or high school might collaborate across their shared courses from Spanish I to AP Spanish. This format will also often require some level of electronic teaming if the teachers involved do not work on the same campus.

We have seen successful PLC schools in which some elective teachers work with other content teams to support interdisciplinary essential standards. For example, at Pioneer Middle School in California, the home economics teacher found that many of her standards regarding healthy eating were perfectly aligned to healthy lifestyle standards in physical education and human biology standards in life science. The home economics teacher made these connections by reviewing the essential standards selected by the core subjects and then seeing if there were strong connections with essential content from her courses.

The focus on 21st century skills offers excellent opportunities to support interdisciplinary teaming around higher-level thinking skills. For example, an interdisciplinary team—that includes elective teachers—can focus on the college-ready skills David Conley (2007) recommends, including:

- Reading and discussing analytically
- Writing persuasively
- Drawing inferences and conclusions from texts
- Analyzing conflicting source documents
- Supporting arguments with evidence
- Solving complex problems with no obvious answer

These essential learning standards are not subject specific. Each teacher on the interdisciplinary team can use his or her unique subject content as the vehicle to teaching these higher-level thinking skills. The team can clearly define these common learning outcomes, discuss effective Tier 1 core instruction, develop common rubrics to assess these skills, and respond collectively when students need additional time and support.

These solutions demonstrate that there is not a one-size-fits-all approach to forming teams with elective teachers. We highly discourage administrators from arbitrarily assigning elective teachers together on a team and using the list of Conley's (2007) essential standards to justify the decision. For example, we have visited schools that assign core subject teachers to course-specific teams but then throw together the elective and physical education teachers onto a "team" and tell them to focus on writing across the curriculum. While this focus might be meaningful for some elective teachers, it is unlikely to be a perfect fit for all. (Physical education teachers told us that their facilities lacked writing materials or the space for students to write.) Instead, the administration should work closely with each elective teacher to determine the best collaborative structure for each educator. The administration has an obligation to be tight about two outcomes: that every teacher will be part of a high-performing team and that the team will focus on the four critical questions of learning in the PLC process. However, the administration must be loose on exactly what team each teacher is on, working with each staff member to find the best possible match to support each person's day job. (Also see page 51, "I have been assigned to an electronic team. How do we team?")

Fostering Collaboration

I have been assigned to a job-alike team with members spread across the district. How do we team?

Teachers who are singletons in their schools can become members of district or regional job-alike teams. They can meet in face-to-face settings periodically, but most often, the team agrees on a common block of weekly time for collaboration so that members can remain in their school settings and use technology to facilitate collaboration. (Also see page 51, "I have been assigned to an electronic team. How do we team?")

I teach three different subjects or courses at our secondary school. Whom should I team with?

We recommend assigning teachers in this situation to no more than two teams. The principal should work with the teacher to determine specifically which team or teams. If the teacher is on two teams, it is critical to schedule collaboration time so the teacher can meet weekly with both teams—instead of attending each team meeting every other week—as it is difficult to be a contributing team member if one misses 50 percent of the team meetings. For the third course or subject, the teacher must honor the team decisions that the teachers make who do collaborate regularly about that course. Our experience is most teachers will gladly honor this work, because when you teach multiple preps, it is helpful to receive support from peers.

I am a school counselor. Whom do I team with?

If a counselor is in a school with more than one counselor, we recommend he or she teams with fellow counselors. For example, counselors would play a critical role in a secondary school that is committed to helping more students access and succeed in rigorous curriculum. The counselor team could establish a SMART goal in that area and work with classroom teachers to identify strategies for persuading students and their parents to assume the challenge of more rigorous curriculum.

Every counselor, whether working alone or with other counselors, should play a critical role in creating and monitoring the school's system of interventions and enrichment. Counselors should receive ongoing information regarding the academic performance of their students and should be lead people in implementing decisions regarding when students should be moved from one level of intervention or enrichment to another. We think of counselors as members of two teams: (1) the intervention team and (2) a liaison to a specific course or grade level. In middle and high school, counselors will also be members of the counseling department.

I am a special education teacher and serve students at almost every grade level. Whom do I team with?

At the elementary level, the special education teacher might join one or two grade-level teams in which his or her caseload is the largest. The teacher should become familiar with intended outcomes for each unit, help develop common assessments, and support students in acquiring essential outcomes and preparing for assessment. He or she could assist the team in analyzing evidence of student achievement, identifying skills or concepts that proved problematic for students with special needs, and offering strategies and materials to address those problems. The teacher could also be instrumental in providing additional time and support for students during blocks of time established for intervention and extension.

At the secondary level, assuming there are multiple special education teachers, those teachers would be members of two teams—a course-specific content team and the special education team. Assignment to a content team should be based on analysis of the courses in which special education students have traditionally struggled. A special education teacher could serve on a content team and provide special education expertise to his or her content colleagues. The teacher should become familiar with the intended outcomes of every unit and the various assessments the team will use to monitor student learning. The teacher should also provide the team with strategies and materials designed to support special education students in their learning. That same teacher would then liaise between the content team and his or her special education colleagues. The teacher could help those colleagues understand key skills and concepts of the unit and the manner in which students will demonstrate their proficiency. He or she is responsible for equipping the other special education teachers to prepare their students to succeed in the course.

I am the library specialist. Whom do I team with?

Library specialists play an important role in the teaching and learning process for students and staff throughout a school building. We strongly and enthusiastically endorse the position that school librarians should teach important skills and concepts to students *and* collaborate on meaningful teams. The American Association of School Librarians (2009) has endorsed the PLC at Work process as a way to foster collaborative partnerships for all members of the learning community.

Most often, however, a single librarian serves an entire school community, and it would be impossible for a single librarian to meet with every team every week, just as it would be impossible for a single art, music, physical education, or technology teacher to meet with every team every week. Therefore, at least one of the following options for meaningful teamwork should resonate with school librarians.

- **District or regional team:** This is a district or regional job-alike team with other school librarians. The team can meet face to face periodically, but most often, the team agrees on a common block of weekly time for collaboration so that members can remain in their school settings and use technology to facilitate collaboration.

- **Logical links team:** This is a grade-level team that is pursuing a SMART goal and outcomes linked to a librarian's areas of expertise. A librarian could select one or two teams each year to co-labor with on a regular basis. Leaders should build schedules to accommodate his or her participation.

- **Vertical team:** This is a team with job-alike colleagues in the district. If the proximity of the schools does not allow for face-to-face meetings, team members use available technology to facilitate electronic collaboration.

I have been assigned to an electronic team. How do we team?

Two keys to effective teams are preserving sacred time for members to collaborate and providing clarity regarding the right work. Electronic teams must address both of these keys. Teammates must establish a time each week when all members are available to engage in the PLC process. This often requires coordination of teaching schedules so that members share common preparation periods. For example, educators in a rural district in Utah with four very small high schools found it difficult to collaborate because their schools operated under different schedules, including different start and end times in the teacher workday. The central office worked with the principals to establish the same schedule for the four schools. The principals then worked together to ensure that the course-specific teachers in each of the four schools shared a common planning period. The teams selected one day each week to use for their collaborative team meeting. They met using Skype and addressed all the issues school-based teams would address, including discussing evidence of student learning with their colleagues and sharing strengths and addressing concerns as a team.

Members of electronic teams can also use VoiceThread and sites that allow members to share ideas, questions, and materials at their convenience. In that case, a team norm would be for each member of the team to commit to check those sites and respond within a designated time frame (for example, within forty-eight hours).

Proximity does not guarantee a great collaborative team. Teachers can be in rooms next to one another and still work in isolation. Distance does not negate the possibility of powerful collaboration. Research teams with members in different countries have won the Nobel Prize. The technology is available to help educators work as members of powerful virtual collaborative teams if they are willing to coordinate their schedules and focus on the right work. (Also see page 49, "I have been assigned to a job-alike team with members spread across the district. How do we team?")

Who should decide teacher team assignments?

Team assignments are determined by teaching assignments, not by individual preferences. The team structures most likely to have a positive impact on student achievement are common courses at the secondary level and common grade levels at the elementary level. All geometry teachers should be on the geometry team. All second-grade teachers should be on the second-grade team.

For teachers who do not fit neatly into this arrangement (for example, singletons), we recommend that the principal work with those individuals to determine a team structure that will be most meaningful for them. For example, in Becky's former elementary school, Boones Mill, the music teacher joined the fourth-grade team and helped students learn about famous Virginians by writing a musical about them. A junior high band director may prefer to work on a vertical team with the high school band director to create a strong band program. Some districts carve out time each week for all the art teachers to come together to focus on the four critical questions. An AP statistics teacher may ask to join an electronic team devoted to that course.

I am a site administrator. Whom should I team with?

A foundational consideration for teams in a PLC is creating meaningful teams, teams that make sense—teams that focus on similar issues and concerns around the fundamental purpose of high levels of learning for all. Thus, the same criterion applies here—site administrators should collaborate with other site administrators who have a similar role and share similar responsibilities. We offer suggestions for the nature of this collaboration in chapters 3 and 10 of *Learning by Doing, Third Edition* (DuFour et al., 2016).

Site administrators (principals and assistant principals) should also collaborate with a guiding coalition of teacher leaders at their sites. Effective principals can harness the positive power of teacher leadership by creating a guiding coalition in their schools. See the response to "What is a guiding coalition?" in chapter 1 (page 21) of this book for important information on the guiding coalition.

I work at the district office. How do we form teams?

Just as teacher teams should consist of teachers who teach the same or similar content, district office teams should comprise people who share the same or similar work. The key to creating effective teams is to ensure that team members share common work.

Because of the nature of the work at the district level, people may be on more than one team, depending on the tasks they undertake and the size of the district. In addition, team members may serve in different capacities on different teams—taking the lead in some cases and serving in a more advisory or resource role in others. Again, the issue is creating a collaborative workplace in which people cooperate to collectively inquire into best practices, undertake action research to test the effectiveness of various practices and make data-based decisions, and create a culture of continuous improvement. The organizing structure to achieve such a culture may vary from district to district, or even within the same district.

At times, only one person fills a particular role with no apparent team members with whom to collaborate, at least on a regular basis. In these cases, we recommend using technology to form virtual teams with others who are engaged in the same or similar work in other districts. A wide range of organizations throughout the world have formed highly effective teams through the use of technology, and for those who work at the district level, virtual teaming offers a powerful, effective alternative to working alone.

Creating Time to Meet

Why do educators need time to collaborate?

There are five significant reasons why educators need time to collaborate.

1. Leaders in most professions consider time spent in collaboration with colleagues essential to success. The law firm that represented Rick's school district, Adlai E. Stevenson, when he was superintendent required all its attorneys to meet on a weekly basis to review the issues and strategies of the various cases that had been assigned to individual members. Each attorney presented the facts of the case and his or her thoughts on how to proceed. The others offered advice and challenges and shared their experience and insights. The board of education never considered this collaboration inappropriate. In fact, its members would have been very upset if the advice they received had been limited to the perspective of a single person rather than the collective expertise of the entire firm.

   Educators are professionals, and they, too, benefit from the insights, expertise, and collective efforts of a team of colleagues. Collaboration is not a frill; it is an essential element of professional practice.

2. The research base in support of collaboration is extensive both inside and outside of education. The collaborative team has been called the fundamental building block of a learning organization, and the link between a collaborative culture and improving schools is well established. No district should disregard the compelling evidence that collaboration represents best practice *as long as people demonstrate the discipline to collaborate about the right things*. Visit AllThingsPLC to view the "Advocates for PLCs" document (www.allthingsplc.info/articles-research /search-result/view/id,150) to see this research.

3. American educators often face criticism because their students do not score as well as Asian students on international tests. The workweek of Japanese teachers is similar to that of American teachers in terms of the number of hours at work, but the time spent in front of students in the classroom is considerably less (Mehta, 2013). In Japan, it is understood and accepted that a teacher who is working with colleagues to perfect a lesson or review examples of student work is engaged in highly productive activities that have a positive impact on student achievement (Mehta, 2013).

4. Lou Gerstner (1995), the former chairman of IBM, was asked if he felt the key to improving American schools was simply extending the time teachers

spent in the classroom—more time on task, longer school days, longer school years. Gerstner pointed out that the United States has created a system that impacts students for thirteen years (K–12), yet approximately one in every four students who enter the system fails to complete it (that is, he or she drops out). Furthermore, many of those who do complete the system are incapable of doing what the system was designed to ensure they could do. Gerstner insisted that if IBM found that one in every four of its computers failed to reach the end of the assembly line, and many of those that did could not do what the computer was designed to do, IBM would not solve the problem by running the assembly line more hours in the day or more days in the year. IBM would have people sit down together and determine more effective ways to achieve the intended objective.

5. Finally, organizations demonstrate their priorities by how they use their resources. Time is one of the most precious resources in a school. In light of the strong correlation between meaningful collaboration and improved student achievement, it would be disingenuous for any board of education to argue that it wants better results but it is unwilling to provide this essential, cost-neutral resource to achieve them.

How often should teacher teams meet?

We advocate that teachers should meet at least weekly. (See the following answer for details on meeting length.)

How long should each meeting last?

Weekly team meetings should last approximately one hour. Leadership teams should also look for every opportunity to offer extended time for teams to meet. Most schools typically have several days set aside at the beginning of the school year when educators return to school before students arrive. Leadership teams could reserve some of those days for collaborative teams to establish their norms, their SMART goals, their guaranteed and viable curriculum for each unit, and some of the common formative assessments the team will use. Using time this way will have a greater impact on student achievement than listening to a convocation speaker or putting up bulletin boards.

Another way to provide extended time for collaborative team meetings is to devote professional development days to the collaborative team process. Using time for this purpose is one of the most effective ways to provide powerful, job-embedded professional development. Some schools have a practice of hiring substitute teachers each quarter to give teams a half or full day of extended time for collaboration.

When the PLC process is done well, teams will always look for more time to collaborate, and teachers can become very creative in generating ideas to provide that time.

We don't have time in our master schedule to meet. What do we do?

Principals often ask, "How will we find the time to collaborate?" The answer is that you will never *find* time for collaboration. The reality is that most schools already have all the time they are going to get and if principals want more time for collaboration, they must *make* time by changing the daily schedules and routines of their schools. No schedule is carved in stone, and most veteran educators acknowledge that they have worked under a variety of different schedules during their careers. It should therefore be evident to all that they can change schedules.

Some districts provide time for teachers to collaborate through the use of early dismissal or late start days for students, allowing for collaboration while the students are off campus. In many communities, however, changing school schedules is not an option because of busing issues, custodial care, budget constraints, or state mandates regarding instructional minutes each day. Therefore, principals and teacher leaders must be creative in providing time for teachers to collaborate while students are at school without increasing costs or losing a significant amount of instructional time. The resource "Making Time for Collaboration" provides multiple strategies for building collaborative time into the weekly schedule that meet the criteria we have listed. Visit AllThingsPLC (www.allthingsplc.info/files/uploads/makingtimeforcollaboration.pdf) to access it.

You can also contact any of the hundreds of schools featured on AllThingsPLC for information on how they have created time for collaboration.

One of the ways in which leaders demonstrate the priorities of their organization is through the allocation of resources. In schools, one of the most precious resources—second only to human resources—is time. The schedule reflects the priorities of the school. If principals and superintendents hope to foster a collaborative culture, it is *imperative* that they create schedules that provide time for teachers to co-labor with their teammates.

Where can we find sample schedules for teacher collaboration?

Sample elementary and secondary schedules are posted on AllThingsPLC (www.allthingsPLC.info) in the Tools and Resources section. In addition, many of the model PLCs featured on AllThingsPLC on the Evidence of Effectiveness page have posted downloadable versions of their master schedules in the Resources sections of their entries. All these schools also describe in their narratives how they provide teachers with collaborative time. Virtual visitors to the model sites may access a school's contact information on the first page of the entry and request more information about the school's schedule and practices.

If a school is banking minutes to create collaboration time, is it better to have a late start or an early dismissal to provide collaborative time?

Although we can cite no research supporting one of these options over the other, our experience leads us to prefer the late start, particularly for secondary students. Imagine a school attempting to decide between pushing the start of instruction back from 8:15 to 9:00 a.m. or shortening the school day to 2:00 rather than 2:45 p.m. With the late start, students who can drive or carpool typically choose to sleep in. Buses can pick up those who rely on bus transportation at the usual time to avoid inconveniencing their parents. Supervising those students when they arrive to school would fall to nonteachers—administrators, counselors, deans, and clerical staff—who can schedule their collaborative meetings while classes are in session. The supervision required of sleepy teenagers is typically very minimal. Release those same students at 2:00 p.m., and they have much more energy and a far greater opportunity to wreak havoc on the community.

At the elementary level, we still would recommend the late start, less because of the energy levels of students and more because of the energy levels of their teachers. It is typically more difficult to summon the necessary vigor after teaching the entire day than upon entering the building in the morning.

The most important advice we can offer for all schools on this question is that whether you choose a late start or an early dismissal, *do not inconvenience the community you serve*. Doing so will cause a backlash against teacher collaboration, not because parents are opposed to your collaborating with colleagues but because you are creating transportation and childcare problems for families. For example, if your school delays bus pick-up for elementary students by forty-five minutes one day each week, it disrupts parents' work or childcare schedules. Buses should run their regular routes so parents are not inconvenienced, and the school should provide options for students who arrive to the campus early or remain beyond the end of the instructional day.

Planning for Teacher Team Meetings

Should teacher teams have an identified team leader? If so, how should we select the team leader?

We strongly advocate that teams with four or more members have a designated team leader. Team leaders serve as liaisons between the team and the administrators who are monitoring and supporting the collaborative, learning-focused work. Team leaders ensure they and their teammates:

- Make collective commitments (generate norms)

- Paint and analyze the team's data picture

- Establish the team's SMART goals

- Develop, monitor, and evaluate the team's action plan to achieve the goals

- Study, discuss, and generate products aligned with each of the eighteen critical issues for team consideration (see chapters 3 and 5 of *Learning by Doing, Third Edition* [DuFour et al., 2016], or the "Critical Issues for Team Collaboration" document on www.allthingsPLC.info).

We have seen schools approach the selection of team leaders in several different ways. For example, some PLC schools employ the following strategies.

- They create a job description and an application and interview process. Interested teachers apply for clearly defined roles, and school administrators interview them about the responsibilities they will be asked to fulfill. At the conclusion of the interviews, the administrators select the teacher leaders they perceive will be successful in the position.

- They allow team members to appoint or elect a team leader within clearly defined selection parameters; for example, team leaders:

  - Must have experience in teaching the content of the team's course or grade level

  - Have at least one year of teaching experience

  - Must not already be fulfilling another teacher-leader position in the school

- They establish roles and responsibilities for each member of the team and rotate positions over time.

Regardless of the selection process, it is vitally important that the administrators provide team leaders with the necessary support, training, and resources to be successful in what they are being asked to do.

Who should determine the agenda for teacher team meetings—the administration or each teacher team?

The nature of this question suggests a traditional approach to decision making: Who will have the power to decide? It suggests the lines are drawn and there is a power struggle. In a PLC, decisions are made not on the basis of power but through *learning* together—by building shared knowledge about the most promising practice. The question as posed should also raise a red flag because it frames the issues in terms of the *Tyranny of Or* rather than the *Genius of And* (Collins & Porras, 1997). It asks if teachers *or* administrators should make the decision. The *Tyranny of Or* approach leads to winners and losers. The *Genius of And* approach seeks the best of both worlds and a win-win result.

Both teachers and administrators should be able to agree that it would be unreasonable for a district to provide staff with a resource as precious as time and then to be indifferent as to how they use that resource. That does not mean, however, that the administration needs to dictate the agenda or topics of every team meeting. Both sides should be able to agree that if teachers do not use the collaboration time for the purpose intended (that is, if they don't collaborate on the right work), there will be no gains in student achievement. Both sides should also agree that teams must become self-directed if they are to sustain the process when a principal leaves a school and that micromanaging does not contribute to sustainability.

We have found that the best approach is for principals and team leaders to agree on the work to be done, establish a timeline for completion, and clarify the evidence that teams will present to demonstrate their work. Then give the teams autonomy to determine the agenda for any particular meeting. When teams are unable to provide tangible evidence that they are making progress on the right work, then the administration can step in to help them address whatever problems they are experiencing.

For example, chapter 3 in *Learning by Doing, Third Edition* (DuFour et al., 2016), and the "Critical Issues for Team Collaboration" document on AllThingsPLC (www.allthingsPLC.info) feature the eighteen critical issues we contend represent the "right work" for collaborative teams in a PLC. Some of these issues are addressed annually, some are recursive, and some are repeated over and over as part of a continuous cycle. For example, a team will create team norms and annual SMART goals only once. They will establish the essential outcomes for a unit, agree on pacing, and develop preassessments and common formative assessments repeatedly for each unit.

Our advice is to have the principal and team leaders agree on a timeline for when teams will do the work, create clear expectations regarding the product they will create, and let teams set their own agendas until there is evidence that they are struggling. For example, the timeline might look like this.

1. **After your second meeting:** Present your team norms and SMART goal.

2. **After your fourth meeting:** Present the essential outcomes for your course and for the first unit you are teaching.

3. **After your sixth meeting:** Present your first common assessment.

4. **After your eighth meeting:** Present your analysis from a common assessment, including areas of celebration, areas of concern, and your strategies for proceeding.

5. **After your tenth meeting:** Present the essential skills for the next unit and a preassessment for those skills.

In this instance, the team performs the first step once during the year. The other steps could occur for each unit. The team members understand the expectations for providing evidence of their work, but they have some latitude in what happens at any given meeting.

The approach we are presenting works best when leadership is widely dispersed, so we recommend that principals work directly with team leaders to clarify expectations and help resolve problems, task by task. It also demands that principals demonstrate *reciprocal accountability*, Richard Elmore's (2003) phrase for the premise that if leaders are going to hold others accountable for completing work and achieving goals, then leaders are accountable for providing everything those people need for success. We have listed the questions and issues that a leadership team must be prepared to answer for each product it asks a team to create in chapter 3 of the third edition of *Learning by Doing* (DuFour et al., 2016). We also provide the resources to help answer those questions in the same book.

Should administrators attend teacher team meetings?

Generally, it is absolutely imperative that administrators have a process for monitoring the work of teams, but monitoring does not require their attendance at every team meeting. Administrators should attend team meetings only when invited or when it becomes evident that a team is struggling to generate high-quality products that demonstrate the team is making progress on the right work. (See the answer for "Who should determine the agenda for teacher team meetings—the administration or each teacher team?" on page 59.) We urge principals to think of team monitoring in the same way teachers use differentiated instruction. Some teams will embrace the collaborative team process, understand the work to be done, and establish a highly effective working relationship. These teams need a minimum of administrative supervision. Principals should stay out of these teams' way and periodically ask what they can do to further support the teams. Some teams will experience confusion and conflict. They will need more direct administrative support and the presence of administrators at their meetings until they become more comfortable with the process. The ultimate goal, however, is for the teams to become self-directed.

Should teacher teams be required to submit meeting minutes?

There is no research about the impact of minutes and agendas on student learning that we are aware of. In our experience as administrators, if teams felt it would be beneficial to create an agenda and have minutes, then they did so; however, if they preferred not to, they didn't. Put in PLC language, we were loose on minutes and agendas.

What we were tight on, however, was that teams would submit products that should flow naturally from a team engaged in doing the right work. We worked with teacher leaders to establish a timeline for the products, and if a team was unable to generate a product according to the timeline, then we knew the team required some assistance, such as clarification of the task, examination of samples of the product in question created by other teams, or mediation of conflict.

The products came from the list of eighteen critical questions that are available at AllThingsPLC (www.allthingsPLC.info) in the Tools and Resources section ("Critical Issues for Team Collaboration") as well as in chapter 3 of *Learning by Doing, Third Edition* (DuFour et al., 2016). For example, we would want to see the team's norms, SMART goal, expected learning outcomes for the semester and grading period, key prerequisite skills or vocabulary students would need for success in the upcoming unit, and plan for gathering evidence of whether each student had the necessary skills and vocabulary, and common formative assessments created by the team. Most important, we wanted to see the team's data analysis protocol sheet for each common formative assessment to ensure they were using it to identify students needing help or extension, to share strengths, and to identify areas in which the entire team needed support to help students learn a particular concept. The "Data Analysis Protocol" is also available on AllThingsPLC in the Tools and Resources section and in *Learning by Doing, Third Edition* (DuFour et al., 2016).

Remember the reason you are asking for these products is to see if teams understand the work to be done, if they are getting it done, and the quality with which they are getting it done. This puts you in a position to support teams who struggle. Which will give you better insight into the work of a team—having minutes that say the team wrote a common formative assessment or actually looking at the common assessment?

We contend that you are much better off being loose on minutes and agendas and tight on teams presenting clearly defined products within a designated time frame.

What should be the focus of our team meetings?

Teachers have gathered together in groups for generations. In the best of times, these groups discuss grading practices and gigabytes. In the worst of times, they struggle through awkward conversations about problems outside their control. While issues such as dress codes, field trips, and tardy policies may be school related, they do not represent the kind of work we envision will be the focus of highly effective teams.

Effective teams focus their efforts on responding to the four critical questions of a PLC.

1. What is it we want our students to learn? What knowledge, skills, and dispositions do we expect them to acquire?

2. How will we know our students are learning? What evidence will we gather to ensure students understand the skills and concepts we are teaching?

3. How will we respond when some of our students don't learn?

4. How will we respond when many of our students have already demonstrated proficiency in the skill or concept under consideration?

A powerful tool that elaborates on these questions and clarifies the right work for teams is the section "Critical Issues for Team Consideration" in chapter 3 of *Learning by Doing, Third Edition* (DuFour et al., 2016).

How does a team decide who has responsibility for doing what?

There is no definitive list of which roles must be present on teams. At a minimum, most teams of four or more members designate one person as the team leader or facilitator. Teams will often have a recorder or note taker and usually a timekeeper. Many teams assign someone the role of air traffic controller or process observer and charge him or her with the task of monitoring participation levels or observing how the team conducts meetings.

To be most effective, teams should review roles and responsibilities on a regular basis. Occasionally, individuals take a back seat or expect others to complete important tasks, but teams can prevent this and enhance the likelihood that all members will fulfill their responsibilities when the expectations for each role are clearly and carefully defined.

Creating Team Norms

Should every collaborative team in a PLC create its own collective commitments?

Yes. Commitments can only be made by the individuals who are expected to honor them.

How many norms should a team have?

Less is more in the case of norms. Fewer norms are better than a long laundry list. There should be a sufficient number to describe how team members will work together.

What topics or issues should team norms specifically address?

Teams should create norms that address things like time (punctuality and timeliness), communicating (listening and responding), decision making (inquiry and advocacy), participation (attendance and engagement), and expectations (roles and responsibilities). Norms should focus on the behaviors that promote development of a collaborative culture focused on learning.

In addition to these basics, one of the norms should describe a process for how teams will respond when someone violates a team norm. Here are examples of this last, but very important, norm.

- Give a nonverbal cue that a norm has been violated. Team members might pick up an object (for example, a stuffed animal representing the school's mascot or the face of Norm from the television show *Cheers* mounted to a stick) to signal that a norm has been broken and then proceed to describe how the norm was broken.

- Put the topic (the specific norm) on the next agenda and talk about the impact violating the norm has on the team.

- The team leader or team discusses the problem with the individual who didn't honor the norm in an effort to recommit that person to the norm process.

- Facilitate a conversation with the principal between the team and the person who is violating the norm.

Should norms be reviewed at every meeting?

Team members should review norms and collective commitments at the start of every meeting until they are internalized. It is also a good strategy to check at the end of the meeting to see if any team members want to comment on the team norms. The next section on team norms provides some easy ways to assess whether a team's norms are effective.

How often should a team revise its norms?

At a minimum, teams should revise their norms at the beginning and end of each school year. However, nothing prevents a team from revising its norms. It might become clear during the process of regularly reviewing team norms that it is necessary to respond to a new and unanticipated behavior that has developed on the team. At that point, it is appropriate to add a new norm.

We have agreed on team norms. Now what?

Teams should be careful not to spend too much time figuring out how to work together—it is better to focus on the work; however, it is imperative that teams regularly revisit, review, and reinforce the values and commitments the members made to the team and each other. Reinforcing norms does not have to be complicated, but it is important to understand that once the team has created norms, they must reinforce them. We offer several strategies to help teams reinforce their norms in chapter 3 of *Learning by Doing, Third Edition* (DuFour et al., 2016).

It is imperative that teams pause from time to time throughout the school year and reflect on three items: (1) what the team has been doing that members should do more of, (2) what the team has been doing that members should do less of, and (3) what new norms the team should create to improve their effectiveness.

How should a team handle norm violations?

One of the most important norms a team can establish in its initial effort to clarify its commitments regarding its collective work is to identify how the team will address violations of the norms. Having norms does not eliminate conflict, but it does serve as a constant reminder of commitments and provides a basis for discussion when conflict arises. Clarifying what will happen when members violate norms establishes the rules of engagement at the beginning of the collaborative team process before conflict emerges.

What is a norm check?

The only norms that matter for a team are the ones that the team is willing to enforce. A *norm check* is a protocol a team uses to acknowledge that a member has violated a team norm. The team agrees on an action—most often some sort of nonverbal cue—that team members can use when they feel a team norm has been broken. The cue might be a hand signal or small signs distributed to each team member. Whenever a teammate uses the signal, the team briefly stops the meeting to acknowledge the concern and refocus on following the team's collective commitments.

What if a teammate purposely, willingly, and consistently breaks team norms?

Once again, a team should establish how it will address violations of norms at the very outset of team formation. It should then adhere to the process it has established when violations occur. Typically, teams handle violations with low-level reminders, such as signals, and teams often establish one person to provide reminders. If the violations persist, the team leader should meet with the individual in an attempt to have that person recommit to the team and its norms. The team may opt for a collective intervention with the colleague to seek an explanation for the behavior, to articulate the concerns regarding the behavior, and to ask for the changes necessary to honor the team norms. If the team's efforts fail to resolve the issue, the team must ask the administration to intervene. At that point, the administration must direct the person who is violating the commitment to begin immediately acting in accordance with the PLC process. The administration should spell out, very specifically, the behaviors the individual must exhibit and make it clear that any further violations will result in disciplinary action. From that point on, the administration must closely monitor the individual's behavior. Nothing will destroy the PLC process faster than unwillingness to address—directly and emphatically—behavior that consistently violates the process.

What is the difference between norms and protocols?

The terms *norms* and *protocols* are often used interchangeably, but they serve different purposes on teams. Norms and protocols are both important. The best teams understand the differences and use each to enhance collaboration on the team.

Some schools refer to *norms* as the standards of behavior by which we agree to operate while on a particular team. Others like Kegan and Lahey (2001) describe norms as "commitments" (p. 13) and "public agreements" (p. 103) among members of a team. Any way you define them, norms enhance productivity, promote collaboration, and create the environment for a successful experience among adults in the school.

Protocols outline the process that teams will use to accomplish a task or produce a product. A protocol consists of agreed-on guidelines that promote efficient and effective conversations about teaching and learning.

What are some of the benefits of using protocols?

We know that telling teams to "go forth and collaborate" is an ineffective way to build a collaborative culture in schools. We also know that teams are more productive when they are purposeful and intentional around their collaborative practices. Effective teams simply refuse to leave the effectiveness of their team meetings to chance.

When principals ask how they can help teams become more intentional—or, said another way, "How can we raise the IQ (intentionality quotient) of our collaborative teams?"—we encourage them to look to protocols as a way to leverage more productive team meetings. Protocols offer a terrific tool to accomplish the goal of raising a team's intentionality by matching specific processes to the different tasks of collaborative teams.

The use of protocols:

- Creates structures that promote development of positive collaborative relationships

- Ensures there are opportunities for more balanced participation of all team members

- Makes it easier for teams to tackle difficult tasks and to ask challenging questions

- Ensures equity in the way each team member participates in team meetings

- Promotes more in-depth and insightful dialogue about ways to improve teaching and learning

Experience has shown that when teams use the right protocols for the right tasks, they are more productive—more effective and efficient—during team meetings.

Are there different protocols for different tasks?

The most familiar use of protocols is for looking at data from common assessments. Most teams do a pretty good job of identifying which students, by name and need, will require additional time and support to be successful. Using protocols can also help teams increase their productivity in at least three other important ways.

1. Teams can support their own learning and help build shared knowledge about best practice by using protocols to promote more frequent

opportunities for professional reading. The most effective teams routinely read and reflect on the latest research as a way to improve their practice. Teams find using protocols to read articles together actually improves discussions of how team members can enhance teaching and learning.

2. Teams find that using protocols to deal with difficult issues and concerns promotes collaboration. The most effective teams use protocols as a way to generate alternatives, which helps team members move from problem finding (complaining) to problem solving (improving their practice). The structure of the protocols in this category makes it easier for teachers to tackle tough issues and have difficult conversations without tearing down relationships.

3. Perhaps the most overlooked use of protocols is as a vehicle to help teachers examine their professional practice. Teams do a pretty good job of using common assessment data to identify students who are and are not proficient, but without a protocol to help them, fewer teams are able to use common assessment data as a way to carefully examine their instructional practice. Protocols in this last category can help accomplish that important task.

For example, teachers find using protocols in the final category helps them decide which activities worked well and should be retained in the unit. Likewise, teams use protocols to decide which strategies need to be tweaked or refined before the unit is taught again. Finally, teams find protocols help them identify which approaches were ineffective and need to be replaced before reteaching the unit. Using protocols to decide which instructional practices to retain, refine, and replace improves instructional practice.

What are some of the characteristics of a protocol?

Protocols share some specific characteristics that set them apart from other strategies that can also enhance the collaborative process. First, protocols provide a structure for a team's conversation. The process of the protocol is outlined in a series of specific and sequential steps that, when followed, keep the team focused and on task. Matching the right protocol to the right task is an important consideration. Choosing the right structure and following the steps as recommended contribute to the effectiveness of the team meeting.

Second, protocols typically include a recommended time frame for the entire process as well as specific time frames for each step of the process. It makes little sense to choose a protocol that requires an hour to complete when the amount of time available for the team meeting is forty-five minutes. Adherence to the suggested time frames contributes to the efficiency of the team meeting.

Finally, a protocol describes the specific roles and responsibilities different people on the team will play. There is no single, definitive list of required roles that applies to all protocols, but most will identify suggested roles to enhance the effectiveness and efficiency of the process. For example, a facilitator or team leader can help ensure that team members follow the steps of the protocol, a timekeeper monitors the time spent on each step, and the recorder will record the outcome of the process.

How can the use of protocols increase the productivity of collaborative teams?

Using protocols helps teams create the conditions that promote more effective conversations around teaching and learning. As Lois Brown Easton (2009) says, in protocols, you'll find "an ideal vehicle for holding the professional conversations that need to occur in PLCs—conversations that will lead to increased student achievement and motivation" (p. 1). In the end, protocols are best viewed as another tool that teacher teams can use to elevate their level of collaboration.

Do you have to like your teammates to be a high-performing team?

Team members don't necessarily have to like each other in order to be high performing, but they must treat each other with respect, dignity, and professional courtesy as they collaborate on behalf of the students they collectively serve. We have seen examples of very high-performing teams whose members never choose to socialize with one another outside of their teamwork. We have also seen examples of teams whose members initially did not like each other, but over time, their collaboration helped them to develop close and lasting friendships.

Is conflict okay on a team?

We do not advocate the kind of knock-down-drag-out battles that border on verbal fisticuffs, but some conflict on teams is healthy. The kind of cognitive conflict that is the hallmark of highly effective teams focuses on issues, not people. *Cognitive conflict* is characterized by disagreement about ideas or approaches, as opposed to *affective conflict*, which tends to become interpersonal, drains the energy of teams, and diverts time and attention away from the right work.

A lack of disagreement among members doesn't signal that a team is more effective; instead, it may be a sign that the members of a team are disinterested in the issue.

How do teams manage conflict so it does not derail team goals?

One way to help teams manage conflict is to clearly define the two different types of conflict and remind everyone that the goal is to encourage cognitive conflict while discouraging affective conflict. (See the previous question for more information about conflict.) Teams that establish reaching consensus—rather than resolving conflict—as their goal begin to shift their mindset in the right direction.

Another way to manage conflict is to use specific advocacy and inquiry processes and protocols to help teams resolve issues and get to an agreement. We offer an example of such protocols in chapter 9 of *Learning by Doing, Third Edition* (DuFour et al., 2016).

What can be done when relationships on the team are toxic or unproductive?

The place to begin when relationships on a team have become toxic or unproductive is to identify the current reality or, as Jim Collins (2001) says, "confront the brutal facts" (p. 70). The way a school or team confronts the brutal facts can mean the difference between being good and becoming great. Confronting the brutal facts is not the same as finding fault.

Toxic and unproductive behaviors will not disappear without a concerted effort by the team to improve their practice. Researchers and educational leaders have contributed to a significant body of work that describes ways to improve collaborative relationships. In a PLC, teachers need not, and should not, accept toxic or unproductive relationships on their teams. As Susan Sparks and Thomas Many (2015) note, "Skills needed to work collaboratively can be learned and practiced" (p. 43).

If team members do not trust each other, can anything be done to build trust?

Principals set the tone for building high-trust relationships in their schools, but they cannot accomplish the task alone. Principals and teachers alike share responsibility for building trust. The key component of trust is aligning one's behaviors with one's words, having the outlook of "We do what we say we will do." This is why establishing and honoring collective commitments is so vital to the PLC process. The single best strategy for creating a trusting environment is clarifying how members will behave and then acting accordingly.

What other resources might we study to learn more about team norms?

The book *Learning by Doing, Third Edition* (DuFour et al., 2016), is an excellent resource for addressing issues associated with developing team norms. Chapter 3 discusses such questions as, "Why should teams develop and use norms?" and provides helpful hints on the development and use of norms to drive the work of teams. Other books that address collaboratively developed team norms and include examples are *Every School, Every Team, Every Classroom: District Leadership for Growing Professional Learning Communities at Work* (Eaker & Keating, 2012) and *Kid by Kid, Skill by Skill: Teaching in a Professional Learning Community at Work* (Eaker & Keating, 2015).

Additional resources are available on AllThingsPLC (www.allthingsPLC.info). This website contains a number of blogs that focus on the issue of using and developing team norms, as well as information about dozens of schools and districts that have successfully implemented the PLC process. Each of these schools relies on team norms to guide how teams work day in and day out. The site includes contact information for each featured school.

Finally, members of PLCs do not overlook the power of learning from each other, or, in other words, gaining shared knowledge. Teacher teams and administrators should share team norms with each other and engage in deep, rich discussions about how they developed the norms, how they use them, and importantly, their effectiveness.

Should administrators monitor the work of teams, and if so, how?

Administrators *must* monitor the work of teams. In most organizations, what gets monitored gets done. Furthermore, leaders demonstrate their priorities by what they pay attention to. A principal who is inattentive to the work of teams sends the message that their work is not important.

Imagine a K–5 elementary school in which teachers are assigned to grade-level teams and each team consists of four members. For the sake of this example, each teacher earns $45,000 per year. Now imagine each team has at least one hour each week to work together collaboratively. If the teacher salaries are broken down into hourly pay, the community will invest tens of thousands of dollars in the collaborative team process each year. It would be irresponsible for any principal to neglect monitoring that process to ensure the investment benefits both students and adults.

However, there is a difference between monitoring and micromanaging. The best way for a principal to monitor a team's use of its time is to ask the team to produce —to generate products that flow from the natural dialogue of a team that is focused on the right work. (See "Who should determine the agenda for teacher team meetings—the administration or each teacher team?" on page 59 for more on the specifics of this approach.)

Should collaboration be optional?

Teachers work in isolation from one another. They view their classrooms as their personal domains, have little access to the ideas or strategies of their colleagues, and prefer to be left alone rather than to engage with their colleagues or principals. Their professional practice is shrouded in a veil of privacy and personal autonomy and is not a subject for collective discussion or analysis. Their schools offer no infrastructure to support collaboration or continuous improvement, and in fact, the very structure of their schools serves as a powerful force for preserving the status quo. This situation will not change by merely encouraging teachers to collaborate, but will instead require embedding professional collaboration in the routine practice of the school.

Sound familiar? These are the conclusions of John Goodlad's (1983) study of schooling published in *Phi Delta Kappan*. Unfortunately, these findings have been reiterated in countless studies from that date to the present. The reason for the persistence of this professional isolation—not merely of teachers but of educators in general—is relatively simple: the structure and culture of the organizations in which they work haven't supported, required, or even expected them to collaborate.

Attempts to promote collaboration among educators inevitably collide with the tradition of isolation. Defenders of this tradition argue that professional autonomy gives each educator the freedom to opt in or out of any collaborative process. We have searched for the dictionary that defines a *professional* as one who is free to do as he or she chooses. We can't find it. In fact, collaborating effectively with others is a condition for membership in virtually all professions.

When schools are organized to support the collaborative culture of a PLC, classroom teachers continue to have tremendous latitude. Throughout most of their workdays and workweeks, they labor in their individual classrooms as they attempt to meet the needs of each student. But the school will also embed processes into the routine practice of its professionals to ensure they co-labor in a coordinated and systematic effort to support the students they serve. Educators will be *required* to work interdependently in the pursuit of a common purpose and common goals. They will be expected to share their expertise with one another and make that expertise available to all the students the team serves. They will establish clear benchmarks and agreed-on measures to monitor progress. They will gather and jointly examine information regarding student learning to make more informed decisions and to enhance their practice. They will not have the opportunity to opt out, because the entire structure of the school will be designed to ensure that they collaborate with their colleagues.

More than a quarter century has passed since Goodlad (1983) warned that overcoming the tradition of teacher isolation will require more than an invitation. We must do more than exhort people to work together. In order to establish schools in which interdependence and collaboration are the new norm, we must create the structures and cultures that *embed* collaboration in the routine practices of our schools, ensure the collaborative efforts focus on the right work, and support educators as they build their capacity to work together rather than alone.

How do we balance team accountability and teacher autonomy in a PLC?

Consider for a moment what a PLC is tight about in regard to teachers' responsibilities to their teammates.

- Work in a job-alike team so the collaborative work supports the teachers' individual classroom efforts.

- Meet with your teammates weekly, usually for an hour per week.

- Agree to identify a limited number of essential standards that all students must learn in your shared grade, subject, or course.

- Agree on how students will demonstrate proficiency and how the team will commonly assess these essential standards.

- Collaboratively review common assessment data to guide the team's next steps in helping all students learn the essential standards.

- Work collectively to intervene and extend student learning.

- Use common assessment results to inform and improve individual teacher and collective team practice.

That's all. This means most teachers will work individually in their own classroom a vast majority of each school day. Teachers retain a great deal of autonomy with their daily and weekly unit plans, as well as with the instructional practices they use to teach essential curriculum. Because the team focuses its collaboration time, common assessments, and interventions on the standards that the team deems essential, that means individual teachers have significant autonomy on how to prioritize, teach, and assess the rest of the curriculum. Finally, when PLC collaboration is done well, the team's collective efforts should help team members' daily efforts in their individual classrooms.

So, when some teachers say that the PLC process is infringing on their professional autonomy, we respectfully challenge that claim with this question: Considering the level of teamwork versus personal autonomy we just described, how much more autonomy should a professional teacher require? Teachers are not independent contractors, nor are they hired to only serve the students assigned to their class. Schools are not antique malls, with each teacher renting a booth and selling his or her individual wares. And as professionals, we are obligated to use practices proven to serve the best interest of our clients—in this case, our students. There is no research to support the proposition that the more autonomy a teacher has, the more students learn. Most professionals are not granted 100 percent autonomy to practice their craft. There is a very reasonable balance of team responsibility versus individual autonomy in the PLC process. In fact, most schools that begin to reap the benefits of the PLC process find their teachers requesting more time to work together and collaborate, not less.

Does merit pay align with the collaborative team concept?

It most emphatically does not! Merit pay works against the interdependence, mutual accountability, and collaboration essential to PLCs that represent best practice in our profession. There is inevitably a cap on the percentage of teachers who can qualify for merit pay. For example, a 25 percent cap ensures that 75 percent of the staff will fail to qualify. Organizations create zero-sum games, where in order for some of their members to win, others must lose, which fosters internal competition, discourages cooperation and mutual assistance, and works against organizational effectiveness. A competitive culture makes the sharing of information and the mutual development of skills very unlikely because it is so counter to individual self-interest.

Why would I, as an individual teacher, share my effective strategies with colleagues if by doing so I risk no longer standing out as exemplary and thus will no longer qualify for merit pay? Why would I help students in another classroom become proficient if by doing so I am taking money out of my own pocket? If I am motivated by money, I will hoard my most effective practices and hope for dismal performances from my colleagues. An organization that expects people to share information, learn from each other, and work collaboratively to enhance overall performance will not rely on a system of internal competition that actually discourages those behaviors.

Another problem with merit pay goes beyond philosophy or sharing of opinions: we have decades of research and evidence demonstrating that it will not help more students learn. A school that claims to value the big ideas of the PLC process, a commitment to higher levels of learning for all students, a collaborative culture and collective effort to support that learning, and the transparency of results essential to improved professional practice will recognize that merit pay runs counter to everything it claims to value.

Fostering
Collaboration

**Additional PLC Resources to Dig Deeper:
Fostering a Collaborative Culture**

- DuFour, R. (2011). Work together: But only if you want to. *Phi Delta Kappan, 92*(5), 57–61. (Available in the Articles and Research section of www.allthingsPLC.info.)

- DuFour, R., DuFour, R., & Eaker, R. (2008). *Revisiting Professional Learning Communities at Work: New insights for improving schools.* Bloomington, IN: Solution Tree Press.

- DuFour, R., & Reason, C. (2016). *Professional Learning Communities at Work and virtual collaboration: On the tipping point of transformation.* Bloomington, IN: Solution Tree Press.

- Erkens, C., Jakicic, C., Jessie, L. G., King, D., Kramer, S. V., Many, T. W., et al. (2008). *The collaborative teacher: Working together as a professional learning community.* Bloomington, IN: Solution Tree Press.

- Ferriter, W. M., Graham, P., & Wight, M. (2013). *Making teamwork meaningful: Leading progress-driven collaboration in a PLC at Work.* Bloomington, IN: Solution Tree Press.

- Hansen, A. (2015). *How to develop PLCs for singletons and small schools.* Bloomington, IN: Solution Tree Press.

Final Thoughts

Knowing what we know about the most promising practices in our field, we know schools that allow educators to opt out of the collaborative process are engaged in a form of educational malpractice.

The preliminary steps to building a collaborative culture call for assigning educators to meaningful teams and providing them with time to collaborate on a regular basis. These are structural issues that are not difficult to resolve. We cannot stress enough, however, that merely providing educators with time to collaborate will do nothing to improve student learning if educators can opt out of the process, function as groups rather than as teams, and not co-labor on the right work. There is a difference between a team and a group. A group can be a loose collection of people who meet periodically to explore a common interest. A team is characterized by three essential characteristics: interdependence, shared goals, and mutual accountability. In terms of the right work, the list of eighteen critical issues that we have repeatedly referenced in this chapter is a valuable tool to keep you engaged in the collective inquiry that leads to higher levels of learning for both students and adults.

Chapter 3

What Do We Want Our Students to Learn?

Responding to the critical question, What do we want our students to learn? is the first step toward ensuring that all students learn at high levels. Responding to this question and identifying essential standards shifts the conversation of a teacher's school, department, or team from an emphasis on teaching to an emphasis on learning. Agreement on what is essential helps teachers focus their time and expertise very specifically in the areas that will be most beneficial for student learning. With agreement in place on what matters most, teachers can be assured that they are applying their energies and professional expertise to what is absolutely essential to student success in the classroom and beyond.

Ensuring that students acquire the standards is different from merely covering the standards. Essential standards identify the *what* of the curriculum, but it remains the teachers' responsibility to determine *how* to present the essential material most effectively. Nothing in the process of identifying the essential standards dictates pedagogy.

Identifying What is Essential

What are essential standards?

Essential standards identify the knowledge, skills, and dispositions all students must acquire as a result of a class, course, or grade level. Essential standards go beyond what is nice to know and identify what students *must* know to be proficient. Students and teachers benefit from a focused, cohesive, and well-articulated curriculum. By agreeing on what is essential, teachers take a significant and fundamental first step toward equipping their students to learn.

What are learning targets?

Learning targets are subsets of a standard, and typically, there are multiple learning targets within a single essential standard. Often described as expectations on the path toward mastery of a standard, learning targets represent the individual concepts and skills embedded within each standard. Identifying the learning targets within a standard is a critical step in promoting a deep understanding of the standard and serves to clarify what teachers should teach and students should learn.

What is an "I can" statement?

A well-constructed "I can" statement clearly states in student-friendly terms what students will learn, and teachers and students understand it. Students cannot track their own progress, assess their own learning, or set specific goals around their own learning without understanding what teachers expect of them. Explaining the intended learning using an "I can" statement at the beginning of a lesson is part of this process.

What are the differences among a standard, a learning target, and an "I can" statement?

The biggest differences among a standard, a learning target, and an "I can" statement are the intended audiences and how each can promote high levels of learning.

District-level content-area teams typically help establish recommended standards. Curriculum committees made up of content experts (teachers) use standards to identify what they should teach and what students should learn, match materials and resources, and monitor progress in a particular subject area across multiple classes, courses, or grade levels.

Collaborative teams for each grade level or course study the recommended standards and establish learning targets for those standards. The learning target identifies the individual skills included within an individual lesson or series of lessons and is the basis for the development of such things as SMART goals, common assessments, and pyramids of intervention.

The intended audience for an "I can" statement is the individual classroom teacher and the student. An "I can" statement is a learning target written in student-friendly language beginning with the words *I can*, and both the teacher and student understand it. The "I can" statement clearly articulates the purpose of the lesson from the students' point of view, helps them grasp why it's important to learn this information, and provides them with success criteria for the lesson.

Aren't all the standards equally important?

All standards are important. However, common sense tells us that some standards are more important—*more essential*—than others. The fact that some standards have more questions on high-stakes assessments, such as state assessments, is evidence of this fact. And, the fact is, all teachers spend more time on some standards than others. Therefore, the key issue is whether to leave the decision of how much instructional time and focus should be given to particular standards up to individual teachers, or to engage collaborative teams to clarify and add meaning to each standard and allocate the appropriate amount of time to reasonably teach each standard. Which is more effective? The answer is clear—the collaborative work of teacher teams. Otherwise, student outcomes depend solely on the teacher to whom students are assigned.

The state requires us to teach all the standards, so why identify essential standards?

When teams of teachers collaboratively determine which standards are the most important—the most essential—they are then able to make some other very important decisions that give focus and specificity to their work. For example, they can collaboratively decide roughly how much time they will allocate within the academic year to reasonably teach a specific standard—especially the more important ones.

Here is a way to think about the appropriate amount of instructional time. If you were to fill a glass beaker to the top with rocks, it would not truly be full because you could then sprinkle gravel around the big rocks to the very top of the beaker. But it still would not be full because you could pour sand around the gravel and big rocks to the top of the beaker. Would it be full? No, because you could pour water to the brim of the beaker. Now, here's the point: this demonstration does not work in reverse. If you fill a beaker to the brim with water, you cannot add sand, gravel, and then big rocks. The same is true with planning for the academic year. If teachers spend all their time on the little rocks (the less important standards), they will be unable to later find the necessary time to effectively teach the big rocks (the more important, essential standards).

Merely providing teachers with a copy of the state standards for their grade level does not ensure all students will have access to a guaranteed curriculum that can be taught in the amount of time available for teaching. Teachers may ignore the standards, assign different priorities to the standards, vary dramatically in how much time they devote to the standards, see huge discrepancies in what the standards look like in terms of student work, and possess significant differences in their ability to teach the standards. The goal is to ensure teachers commit to providing all students with access to the same knowledge and skills. Handing out documents does not accomplish that goal. It can only be achieved when teachers, the people who are called on to implement the curriculum:

- Collectively study the standards

- Agree on priorities with the standards

- Clarify how the curriculum translates into specific student knowledge and skills
- Establish what proficient work looks like
- Establish pacing guidelines or guides
- Perhaps most important, commit to one another that they will actually teach the agreed-on curriculum

Shouldn't we teach all the standards to mastery?

We should teach all *essential* standards to mastery, but not all standards are essential, and thus, not all standards require the same level of emphasis.

An insistence that every standard is equally important, and thus, we should teach every standard forces teachers to abandon deep, meaningful mastery of the essential standards in favor of broad, superficial coverage. We reject the notion that covering all the standards is an acceptable alternative to ensuring students learn the essential standards.

What criteria should we use to determine what is essential?

Teachers at Germantown High School in Germantown, Tennessee, adapted the earlier work of Larry Ainsworth (2013) to create the R.E.A.L. criteria (readiness, endurance, assessed, and leverage). They use the R.E.A.L. criteria to determine if a standard is essential (Many & Horrell, 2014). A standard is considered essential if it reflects the following characteristics.

- **Readiness:** The standard may be essential if it provides students with essential knowledge and skills necessary for success in the next class, course, or grade level.
- **Endurance:** The standard may be essential if it provides students with knowledge and skills that are useful beyond a single test or unit of study.
- **Assessed:** The standard may be essential if it is likely to be assessed on upcoming state and national exams.
- **Leverage:** The standard may be essential if it provides students with knowledge and skills that will be of value in multiple disciplines.

If a standard aligns with these criteria, teachers should consider it an essential standard and teach it to mastery.

Is the goal to create a prioritized list of standards?

The goal of identifying essential standards is *not* to create another list; rather, the goal is to identify the knowledge, skills, and dispositions all students must acquire. Our colleague Tim Brown encourages teachers to think of the essential standards as a promise they make to students about what students will learn. When teachers view standards as promises to keep instead of lists to make, they approach the task of identifying the essential standards in a whole new light.

Teacher teams should not create a prioritized list from top to bottom. Instead, the priority should be on first identifying the more important standards—the standards for which it is essential that all students demonstrate proficiency—while recognizing students will not become proficient at the same time. Once the team has decided how much time teachers would reasonably need to adequately teach these standards, it can allocate the remaining time to the less important, smaller standards.

Homing In on the Specifics

How many essential standards should teacher teams select?

We recommend teacher teams identify eight to ten essential standards per subject, per semester. Teachers need to realize that they will teach more than they assess and assess more than they remediate. Therefore, the number of essential standards will be far fewer than the total number of standards contained in any standards document. Furthermore, each standard contains multiple learning targets, so identifying fewer standards is a more effective strategy than attempting to cover all the standards.

If an essential standard is made up of multiple learning targets, does this count as one standard or more than one?

Although an essential standard consists of multiple learning targets and the sum total of the learning targets only counts as one standard, a different standard may contain a few of the same or similar learning targets. It is not unusual for a specific learning target to also apply to more than one standard. The key is for collaborative teams to break each essential standard into appropriate learning targets with the goal of ensuring that each student will demonstrate proficiency on each learning target in order to ultimately become proficient for each standard.

One way to think of the relationship between standards and learning targets is to think of the concept of sets and subsets in mathematics. Using this analogy, an

Clarifying Learning

essential standard would be a set, and the set is made up of multiple learning targets, or subsets. The important point is this: if students demonstrate proficiency on every learning target (the subset) related to a specific standard, it follows that they should also be proficient at the standard (the set).

Should the selected standards be related to the school or team SMART goals?

Every team should write an annual SMART goal at the beginning of each school year. This goal should require more students to learn the essential standards of their course or subject at higher levels than in the previous year. If the team commits to help more students learn at higher levels, then the members of the team must become crystal clear on the skills, knowledge, and dispositions each student must acquire—the essential standards. Essential standards represent what students should know and be able to do as a result of a class, course, or grade level. As the team identifies the essential standards, unit by unit, it can then develop short-term (unit) SMART goals that call for improvement in student achievement on specific learning targets within an essential standard.

Should an elementary school identify essential standards in all subject areas the first year or focus on just one subject at a time?

Starting with a single subject area during the first year allows elementary teams to narrow the scope of the work and enhance the chances the process will be a success. Ultimately, teachers at the elementary level should identify what is essential in reading, writing, and mathematics. When students exit elementary school with strong literacy and numeracy skills, content specialists at the secondary level are more likely to be successful in teaching them the content.

Where to begin the process of identifying essential standards (with which subject) is a question teachers often struggle with. We recommend elementary schools use student achievement data. Based on assessment results, the faculty should choose the school's greatest area of need, or GAN (the subject area where student performance is weakest), as opposed to the greatest area of comfort, or GAC (the subject where student performance is strongest). If student achievement is lowest in mathematics, teachers should focus the work of identifying essential standards on mathematics. By having the entire school focus initially on the same subject area, teams are able to establish a strong scope and sequence and assist one another when a problem arises in teaching a particular concept. At the secondary level, the identification of essential standards should be course specific. Thus, all biology teachers would work to establish their standards, all algebra teachers their standards, and so on.

What resources will a teacher team need to determine essential standards?

Teams will need access to the standards documents themselves from the state and district levels, any locally or commercially developed pacing guides, recommendations from national or state content groups, relevant examples from the publishers of curriculum materials, and recent assessment results and student achievement data.

How long should it take to identify essential standards?

It should not take long for a team to identify the essential standards if they apply the R.E.A.L. criteria (Many & Horrell, 2014) to each standard. (See the answer to "What criteria should we use to determine what is essential?" on page 78 for more information on R.E.A.L. criteria.) We recommend that the school provide a team with a full day to focus on the task and that the school provide immediate support to any team that is unable to complete it by the end of that day. Remember that every day a team works without the benefit of agreement on the essential standards is another day that students are subject to an educational lottery in which what they learn is dependent on the teacher to whom they are assigned.

What do we do with standards that we deem nonessential?

Teams will teach more than they test but should never test what they have not taught. Their primary focus must be on ensuring every student becomes proficient on standards that they have deemed essential. If time permits, they can certainly address other standards as well.

Examining the District's Role

What is a guaranteed and viable curriculum?

A *guaranteed and viable curriculum* gives students access to the same essential learning outcomes regardless of who is teaching the class, and it can be taught in the time allotted (Marzano, 2003). Clarity regarding essential standards is a prerequisite for a guaranteed and viable curriculum.

What if our district has already identified essential standards? Should each school or teacher team still answer the "learn what" question?

Identification of essential standards promotes the development of a guaranteed and viable curriculum that is a shared responsibility between the district and teachers. There is virtually no chance of achieving the goal of a guaranteed and viable curriculum, however, if teachers—those most essential in providing the guarantee—are not involved in the process of identifying the essential standards.

The district, in consultation with teachers, carries the primary responsibility for the identification of certain aspects of the curriculum all students will be expected to know and be able to do regardless of which school or individual classroom the student is assigned to. A curriculum cannot be guaranteed if every school—or every classroom within a school—chooses to teach a different set of essential standards. A child's zip code must not determine his or her destiny.

Teacher teams, in consultation with the district, have the responsibility to ensure the guaranteed curriculum is viable by determining whether there is sufficient time within the regular school day and school year to teach what the district has identified as essential. A curriculum is not viable if there are too many standards for teachers to teach to mastery. The goal is not to cover the curriculum but rather to ensure that students master the intended outcomes of the curriculum. Teams also play an important role in translating standards into the various learning targets that make up the standard.

Thus, district-level support is a necessary but insufficient condition for the implementation of a guaranteed and viable curriculum. Since teachers are the ones who will ultimately implement the curriculum, they must have a role to play in the curriculum process. It is this dynamic tension between the district and the team that creates the guaranteed and viable curriculum. The individual teacher, acting in isolation, plays no role in the creation of a guaranteed and viable curriculum.

Our district has purchased a new series of textbooks to ensure a consistent curriculum across schools. Shouldn't the textbook determine the curriculum?

The textbook is not the curriculum; it is a tool to help deliver the curriculum. Even if the district has purchased specific textbooks or other related curriculum materials, identified the essential standards, and developed explicit pacing guides, teacher teams still need to unwrap or unpack the standards.

If teacher teams do not unpack or unwrap the standards, they miss the best opportunity to identify and understand the subtle nuances necessary to design their instructional units, construct valid and reliable common assessments, and create schoolwide and systematic pyramids of intervention. This is an example of where engaging teachers in the process is just as important as the end product they create.

What if teammates can't agree on what is essential for students to learn?

In a PLC, a guaranteed and viable curriculum is one thing that is tight, and agreeing on what students should learn and be able to do is how teams respond to the first critical question of a PLC. Responding to this question is one of the non-negotiables for PLC teams. Reaching agreement on this important question requires that teams reach consensus. Refer to chapter 9 in *Learning by Doing, Third Edition* (DuFour et al., 2016), for more information on how to build consensus in a PLC.

If every team identifies essential course- or grade-level standards, how do we ensure vertical alignment?

Teams should meet face to face with teachers from the class, course, or grade level above and below them to ensure that the essential standards are aligned. Initially, the process of articulating the essential standards may need to occur regularly—even as often as monthly or quarterly—but once the process of aligning the essential standards has been completed, annual opportunities for articulation are sufficient.

What is the district's role in identifying essential standards?

The only way a district can ensure that all students have equal access to the same rigorous curriculum—regardless of the school they attend or the classroom they're assigned—is to engage teachers in a process to identify the essential standards. The district's role is to support the process, provide the resources, and establish a guaranteed and viable curriculum for all students. It is a question of equity.

How often should teams go back and revise their list of essential standards?

Nothing is ever written in stone, but if teachers have committed to identifying the essential standards using the R.E.A.L. criteria (Many & Horrell, 2014; see "What criteria should we use to determine what is essential?" on page 78), they should not need to revise what is essential very often. We have found that annual check-ins to

Clarifying Learning

reconfirm what is essential are sufficient. If a revision to the list of essential standards is necessary, it is often because teachers identified too many standards initially and need to reduce their number.

Should we write essential standards in student-friendly language?

Essential standards are intended for teachers, not students. Teacher teams should unwrap or unpack the essential standards to identify the learning targets and then translate them into "I can" statements that they share with students. The "I can" statements are written in student-friendly language.

How can students use standards, learning targets, and "I can" statements to track their own progress?

The intended audience for essential standards and learning targets are teachers and teacher teams. Teams benefit from tracking whether students have mastered the essential standards and the learning targets contained within them, but neither is intended for students.

Students can use "I can" statements to track their progress both individually and as a class. Using "I can" statements is an effective way for students to ask and answer the questions, "Where do I need to go?" "Where am I right now?" and "What do I need to do to close the gap?"

Do teams also have to agree on common pacing for teaching essential standards?

Since common assessments are based on learning targets derived from the essential standards, it makes sense that teams agree on the pacing of the instruction around those learning targets and essential standards. This pacing does not require uniformity on a daily basis (such as, "We will all be on page 16 on Tuesday"), but it does require agreement on how much time teachers will devote to a particular unit and the day or days when they will administer a common assessment.

Our district has mandated pacing guides. What do we do if our team wants to create our own pacing guide aligned to our site essential standards?

First, teachers should recognize that district leadership has a rightful concern for implementing a districtwide guaranteed and viable curriculum. After all, the curriculum a student receives should not depend on the school he or she attends or the teacher to whom he or she is assigned.

On the other hand, teachers need some looseness or flexibility. If a team feels as if the district pacing guide is too restrictive or that it needs to devote more or less time to particular standards or concepts, team members should make a case with their principal for their desired changes. The case should always focus on the issue of enhancing student success, as opposed to "Here's what we like to teach" or "We've always enjoyed taking this field trip."

Districtwide curriculum and pacing guides are most helpful when stakeholders can view them from both a top-down and bottom-up perspective. They should be seen as an initial attempt to guide (rather than dictate) the work of teams. Teams should then have the latitude to tweak the district plan, as long as they have a rational reason that is in the interest of student learning based on a collaborative analysis of student learning data. If, in the final analysis, the team is able to demonstrate that its decisions have led to high levels of student learning, the debate over pacing should become moot.

Clarifying Learning

Should we identify essential behavior standards?

The purpose of answering critical question one (What do students need to know and be able to do?) is to identify the essential knowledge, skills, and dispositions absolutely essential for future success in school. In addition to academic knowledge and skills, there are academic and social behaviors that are important to student success both in school and beyond. So it would be appropriate and necessary for a learning-focused school to:

- Identify the exact behaviors and scholarly dispositions required for student success
- Agree on what proficiency looks like for each behavior
- Teach the behaviors (in contrast to punishing students for not already possessing them)
- Assess student progress at meeting these expectations
- Systematically intervene when students need additional time and support

Unlike with essential academic skills and knowledge, schools as a whole should determine essential behaviors, rather than team by team, as these are behaviors a school will want to build on across classes and from year to year. Using faculty meeting time or forming a task force can be effective ways to achieve this outcome.

What if, once a team has built consensus on what is essential, a team member does not commit to teaching the curriculum?

It is impossible to provide students with access to a guaranteed and viable curriculum unless those who deliver the curriculum have committed to teaching it. Individual preferences must not trump a student's right to acquire essential knowledge, skills, and dispositions. Research has clearly established that implementing a guaranteed and viable curriculum is one of the most powerful practices for improving student learning, and a learning community is committed to implementing what is known to be best practice. Resistance to teaching the agreed-on curriculum and to collaborating is a failure to implement best practice. For ideas and suggestions on how to deal with resistant staff members, see chapter 9 in *Learning by Doing, Third Edition* (DuFour et al., 2016).

Where can we find examples of how teams have successfully answered the first critical question of a PLC?

Figure 3.1 (page 87) shows an essential standards chart teams use to answer the first critical question of a PLC. Figures 3.2 and 3.3 (pages 88–89) show examples of completed team essential standards. Please note that the examples are more than a prioritized list of standards. They are a result of in-depth conversations to create absolute clarity among team members on exactly what all students must master. This includes the following.

- **A description of the standard:** Often the way standards are written can be confusing and up to interpretation. It is important that team members agree on exactly what the standard means.

- **An example of rigor:** What would it look like if a student has met the standard? What level of rigor must a student demonstrate?

- **Prerequisite skills needed:** What prerequisite skills, knowledge, and academic vocabulary do students need to master the new standard?

- **When it will be taught:** While team members do not need to teach every unit of study in day-by-day, lock-step uniformity, a team must agree to teach essential standards at approximately the same time. Without this coordination, it would be nearly impossible for teams to give common assessments and intervene collectively.

- **Common summative assessment:** What assessments will be used to measure student mastery?

- **Extension standards:** Some students will have already mastered the essential grade-level curriculum. To prepare for answering the fourth critical question of a PLC—What will we do when students already know it?—the team should identify curricular outcomes that can extend the learning for these students.

	What Is It We Expect Students to Know and Be Able to Do?				
Grade: _____	Subject: _____	Semester: _____	Team Members: _____		
Description of Standard	**Example of Rigor**	**Prerequisite Skills**	**When Taught**	**Common Summative Assessment**	**Extension Standards**
What is the essential standard to be learned? Describe it in student-friendly vocabulary.	What does proficient student work look like? Provide an example or description.	What prior knowledge, skills, and vocabulary are needed for a student to master this standard?	When will this standard be taught?	What assessments will be used to measure student mastery?	What will we do when students have already learned this standard?

Essential Standards Criteria

1. **Endurance:** Will this standard provide students with knowledge and skills that are valuable beyond a single test date?

2. **Leverage:** Will it provide knowledge and skills that are valuable in multiple disciplines?

3. **Readiness:** Will it provide students with knowledge and skills essential for success in the next grade or level of instruction?

Sources: Buffum, Mattos, & Weber, 2012; Reeves, 2002.

Figure 3.1: Essential standards chart.

Clarifying Learning

Description of Standard	Example of Rigor	Prerequisite Skills	Common Summative Assessment	When Taught	Extension Skills
What is the essential standard to be learned? Describe it in student-friendly vocabulary.	What does proficient student work look like? Provide an example or description.	What prior knowledge, skills, and vocabulary are needed to master this standard?	What assessments will be used to measure student mastery?	When will this standard be taught?	What will we do when students have already learned this standard?
I can read one-syllable and two-syllable words with short vowels, long vowels, and common prefixes and suffixes.	Examples: a. I can read *return, later, chapter, plugging.* b. I can read a second-grade passage at a rate of 110 words correct per minute.	I can read one-syllable words with consonant digraphs, long vowels, and inflectional endings. I can read *chat, play, cave, deeply.*	Students read second-grade words and passages that include one- and two-syllable words with short and long vowels and with common prefixes and suffixes. Teachers track running records monthly.	Monthly	I can read multisyllable words with Latin suffixes.
I can see patterns when reading and use patterns to read and write new words.	Examples: a. I can read the following: *peach, paw.* b. I can read a second-grade passage at a rate of 110 words correct per minute.	I know vowel and spelling patterns.	Students read grade-level passages on a monthly basis. Teachers take running records and analyze patterns of errors.	Monthly	I can produce a portfolio of words with diphthongs and other special vowel spellings.
I can use syllabication rules when reading.	Examples: a. I can read the following: *v/cv = su/per; vc/cv = sup/per.* b. I can read a second-grade passage at a rate of 110 words correct per minute.	I can identify vowels and consonants. I can understand and apply syllabication rules.	Same as above	Monthly	I can consistently use all six syllable types in decoding words.

Source: Buffum, Mattos, & Weber, 2013, p. 36.

Figure 3.2: Second-grade essential standards chart for reading.

Standard	Standard or Description	Example of Rigor	Prerequisite Skills	Common Summative Assessment	When Taught
2.0 10.0	Students understand and use the rules of exponents. Students multiply and divide monomials.	Simplify: $\dfrac{5x^3 y^7}{10 x y^9}$	Multiplying monomials and polynomials (Chapter 4)	Chapter 4	February
11.0	Students apply basic factoring techniques to second- and simple third-degree polynomials. These techniques include finding a common factor for all terms in a polynomial, recognizing the difference of two squares, and recognizing perfect squares of binomials.	Factor completely: 1. $3a^2 - 24ab + 48b^2$ 2. $x^2 - 121$ 3. $9x^2 + 12x + 4$	Multiplying and dividing monomials and polynomials (Chapter 4 and Chapter 5: Sections 1–3)	Chapter 5	February
12.0	Students simplify fractions with polynomials in the numerator and denominator by factoring both and reducing them to the lowest terms.	Simplify: $\dfrac{x^2 - 4xy + 4y^2}{3xy - 6y^2}$	Factoring by finding GCF, difference of two squares, and trinomials (Chapter 5)	Chapter 6	March
2.0	Students understand and use the operation of taking a root and raising to a fractional power.	Simplify: $\sqrt{16} + \sqrt{8}$	Understanding rational and irrational numbers and prime factoring	Chapter 11, Sections 3, 4, 5	March
14.0	Students solve a quadratic equation by factoring or completing the square.	Solve by completing the square: $x^2 + 4x = 6$	Factoring quadratics (Chapter 5) and simplifying radicals (Chapter 11)	Chapter 12, Sections 1–4, and Chapter 5, Section 12	Late March
21.0	Students graph quadratic functions and know that their roots are the x-intercepts.	Graph and state the x-intercepts: $y = x^2 - 3x - 4$	Solving quadratic equations by factoring, completing the square, and quadratic formula (Chapter 12)	Chapter 8, Section 8 and p. 389	April

Clarifying Learning

Source: Buffum et al., 2013.

Figure 3.3: Second-semester essential standards chart for Algebra 1.

Having a team dig this deeply into a standard takes time and effort. Subsequently, teams do not complete this process for every standard, but instead only complete it for a viable number of standards they deem essential for their students' future academic success.

Additional PLC Resources to Dig Deeper:
What Do We Want Our Students to Learn?

- Ainsworth, L. (2003). *"Unwrapping" the standards: A simple process to make standards manageable*. Englewood, CO: Lead + Learn Press.

- Bailey, K., Jakicic, C., & Spiller, J. (2014). *Collaborating for success with the Common Core: A toolkit for Professional Learning Communities at Work*. Bloomington, IN: Solution Tree Press.

- Reeves, D. (2002). *The leader's guide to standards: A blueprint for educational equity and excellence*. San Francisco: Jossey-Bass.

Final Thoughts

One of the intended benefits of adopting consistent state and national standards was better alignment and added coherence—a more guaranteed and viable curriculum. Policymakers and content groups expected that a common set of standards would generate greater consistency around what was taught from grade to grade and school to school. Unfortunately, rigid adherence to the belief that every standard is essential—thus, every standard must be taught—is actually creating more, not less, variance in classroom curriculum.

For generations, teachers have recognized that not all standards are equally important and routinely have made individual decisions regarding what to teach and what not to teach. However, since the practice of prioritizing standards and identifying what is essential is neither sanctioned nor supported in most districts, teachers are left to figure things out on their own and approach this task without the benefit of consistent criteria. This practice of prioritizing standards based on unique and individually created criteria leads to inconsistent choices by teachers, undermines the consistency of what students experience in classrooms, and denies students their right to an implemented curriculum that is guaranteed and viable.

The truth is that while all the standards are important, some are more important than others. Educators must acknowledge this truth. We can begin to make an important shift by acknowledging what we already intuitively know and supporting collaborative teams' efforts to identify the most essential, high-priority standards in systemic and systematic ways.

Chapter 4

How Will We Know When Our Students Have Learned It?

The second critical question that drives the work of collaborative teams in a PLC is, How will we know when our students have learned the essential standards? This question serves as the linchpin of the PLC process. Before a team can answer it, members must agree on the answer to the question, What do we want our students to learn? Once an assessment has taken place, the team and school turn their attention to the questions, How will we respond to students who have not learned? and How can we extend the learning for students who are already proficient? So the questions that drive the work of a PLC flow up and down from this second critical assessment question.

Because members of a PLC are committed to high levels of learning for every student, they focus on each student's proficiency on each essential standard. In other words, their assessments are designed to provide evidence of learning by the student and by the standard—by name and by need. This attention to each student's learning takes place in the classroom as individual teachers use a variety of strategies to check for student understanding almost minute by minute as they teach. They direct questions to randomly selected students and ask classmates to respond to or expand on the answers. They ask students to write their answer in their notes and do a quick check around the room. They work out signals with students—for example, thumbs-up or thumbs-down—so students can indicate their level of understanding. They use clickers, whiteboards, and exit slips to gather evidence of student learning in real time and make adjustments in instruction based on that evidence. Learning how to use effective formative assessment in the classroom each day should be a focus of professional development for every collaborative team.

The cornerstone of the assessment process in PLCs is *team-developed common formative assessments* administered at least once each unit of instruction. These assessments provide crucial information regarding students who need intervention or extension. Equally important, they allow each member of the team to see how his or her students perform on each skill or outcome compared to other members of the team. This collective analysis of transparent evidence of student learning allows members of the team to share strengths, address weaknesses, and identify areas where the team would benefit from supportive professional development.

Defining Assessment

What is a common assessment?

A *common assessment* is an assessment of student learning that uses the same instrument or a common process using the same criteria to determine the quality of student learning and student work. Teachers administer common assessments:

- To gather evidence of the proficiency of students who are in the same curriculum and who are expected to acquire the same knowledge and skills

- At the same time or within a very narrow window of time

- By two or more instructors

Annual state assessments, district benchmark assessments, advanced placement examinations, and unit assessments created by a collaborative team of teachers are all examples of common assessments.

What is a formative assessment?

A *formative assessment* is an assessment *for* learning used to advance and not merely monitor each student's learning. The assessment informs the individual student of his or her progress in becoming proficient. It also informs the teacher regarding the effectiveness of instruction, student needs, and where to go next in the instructional process. The checks for understanding that individual teachers use daily in the classroom are examples of formative assessments. In a PLC, collaborative teams also use common formative assessments to:

- Identify individual students who need additional time and support in order to become proficient

- Provide those students with targeted interventions that do not remove them from new direct instruction

- Give students an additional opportunity to demonstrate their learning

- Identify proficient students who need their learning extended

- Inform and improve their individual and collective instructional practice by collectively analyzing evidence of student learning

What is a summative assessment?

A *summative assessment* is an assessment *of* learning designed to provide evidence that students have acquired the intended knowledge, skills, and dispositions by a designated time. Summative assessments yield a dichotomy: pass or fail, proficient or not proficient. Additional, timely support is typically not forthcoming. The final examination of a high school course or the state assessment administered to students at the end of the year are examples of summative assessments. However, even short-term quizzes and unit tests can be summative if teachers do not provide students with additional opportunities to demonstrate their learning.

Perhaps the best way to distinguish between summative and formative assessments is to remember that summative assessments give students the chance to *prove* what they have learned. They are not designed to give feedback that is useful to teachers and students during the learning process. Formative assessments give students the chance to *improve* their learning because they receive additional time and support and another opportunity to demonstrate what they have learned.

Which is better—formative or summative assessment?

A balanced assessment process will include ongoing formative assessment in the classroom as part of routine instruction; the regular use of high-quality, team-developed common formative assessments; and summative assessments to ensure student learning endures. It is important that teachers understand the purpose of each assessment and why they use it in their classrooms. There is a substantial research base supporting the notion that both continuous formative assessment in the classroom and team-developed common formative assessments can have a powerful, positive impact on student learning.

What determines if an assessment is formative or summative?

What happens *after* the test determines whether teachers are using it in a formative or summative way. If the assessment ensures students experiencing difficulty receive additional time and support and additional opportunities to demonstrate their learning, the assessment is formative. If additional support is not forthcoming and teachers use the test merely to assign grades, it is summative.

Monitoring Learning

Are formative assessments ever graded?

They can be. Keep in mind that good teachers are constantly assessing student learning as they check for understanding while teaching. They use ongoing checks for understanding, such as directing questions to random students, checking student work during the class, and using whiteboards, clickers, exit slips, and so on. They do not grade these kinds of assessments.

Some assessments are merely meant to give students feedback or to gather evidence of student learning so teachers can make decisions about where to go next with instruction. For example, teachers can give a writing assignment and provide feedback to individual students about how to improve their writing. At the same time, they are looking for common errors that they can address in their instruction. In this case, they do not grade the assessments.

But imagine a team gives a common formative assessment to its students at the end of a unit and that it grades this assessment. The team discovers that twelve students have failed the assessment. Because the team has deemed the skills and concepts of the unit to be essential to student success, these students are *required* to keep working and keep learning during the school's block of time for intervention. The students continue to work at mastering the skill. When the tutor indicates they are ready, teachers reassess them. The students earn a C on the reassessment. At this point, their failing grade should become the C they earned. The test is formative because the students received additional time and support and another opportunity to demonstrate that they have learned.

Consider another student in the class who got a C on the first assessment and is not happy with a C. He, too, would like another opportunity to demonstrate he has mastered the skills and concepts at a higher level and is willing to do some additional prerequisite work to qualify for taking a reassessment. He earns a B on that assessment, and his grade is now a B. Once again, after completing some preliminary requirements, he received another opportunity to demonstrate that he learned at a higher level.

Yet another student earned a C on the first assessment and is happy with her grade. Still another student earned an A on that assessment. In both cases, the assessment would be summative for those students. The point is that the same assessment could be summative for some students and formative for others depending on what happens *after* they take the assessment. For students unable to demonstrate proficiency, the test is formative because they will be *required* to keep working and learning. For students who are willing to do additional work in order to qualify for a reassessment, the test is formative. For students who are satisfied with grades that demonstrated proficiency, the test is summative.

Using Common Assessments

Do all of a teacher team's assessments need to be common assessments?

No. Once again, individual teachers can use a variety of strategies to check for student understanding almost minute by minute while teaching a unit. They can also administer their own quizzes or assignments during the unit to make decisions about where to go next in the unit. At least once each unit, however, the team should administer a common formative assessment that the team members themselves created.

How often should teams give common assessments?

Keep in mind that good teachers constantly assess student learning as they check for understanding while teaching. There does come a time, however, when the team needs to gather evidence of student learning to determine individual student needs and to inform the practice of team members. At that point, the team should administer a common formative assessment. We recommend teams avoid establishing an arbitrary number of these common formative assessments, such as, "We will give an assessment every two weeks or six times per semester." Instead, the team should use at least one common formative assessment for every unit of instruction. The time devoted to units may vary. Some units may require one week, while others may require three weeks. The interval between common formative assessments should depend on the length of the units.

Who should create a team's common assessments?

Collaborative teams of classroom teachers should develop common or interim assessments, either by writing items from scratch or borrowing some items from publishers' tests; released items from state, provincial, and national assessments; or past exams. Teachers can determine the validity of a test by whether it assesses what they intend students to learn. Since collaborative teams in PLCs are called on to answer the question, What is it we want our students to learn in this unit? their members are in a better position to create a valid test than textbook publishers. No one is more familiar with which learning targets were taught and what students should know and be able to do as a result of instruction than the teachers who taught those lessons.

Are teachers qualified to create quality common assessments?

Although teachers have been writing assessments for generations, there is a persistent myth in education that writing valid and reliable assessments is a complex and psychometrically sophisticated task reserved for an academic elite. Keep in mind that team-developed common formative assessments are not intended to be psychometrically precise, but rather should provide teachers and students alike with concrete evidence of what students have mastered and where they are experiencing difficulty. The goal is to write common assessments that provide teachers with timely, actionable data they can use to improve student learning. As Doug Reeves (2007) points out:

> When our purpose is a quick determination of the extent to which students understand skills and concepts, and the equally important purpose of adjusting teaching strategies to help students who have not yet mastered those skills and concepts, then practical utility takes precedence over psychometric perfection. (p. 235)

What matters most is that common assessments reflect what is essential for teachers to teach and students to learn. Teachers would certainly benefit from reading books and articles on how to create high-quality assessments, receiving focused professional development on developing assessments, and studying the nature and format of assessments created by experts. We have seen time and again, however, that the best way to learn how to write high-quality common assessments is to jump in, start writing them, and learn by doing.

Is it okay to use the textbook and purchased assessments as team common assessments?

It is perfectly acceptable to use *items* from textbooks and purchased assessments. Items for common assessments may also come from released item banks, end-of-chapter reviews, state assessments, or previously administered classroom assessments. Assessment items can come from many sources, but teams should include no item on a common assessment unless and until they have reviewed and agreed on it. Keep in mind, however, that the *process* of teachers grappling with the question, How can we gather evidence of student learning? is even more important than the end product (the test). Substituting tests created by others for team-developed common formative assessments removes team members from the process and thus removes them from the learning.

How should common assessment data guide interventions?

One of the most important advantages of common formative assessment is that it allows a team to identify students who need additional time and support on the same skill or concept at the same time. This is essential to an effective system of interventions. If individual teachers are all determining what they will teach, how long they will devote to a topic, how they will assess, and what constitutes proficiency, an intervention system will flounder. In that situation, the system is trying to support students who are learning different skills and concepts at different times. Students are sent to intervention because they are "failing algebra." By using common formative assessments, the intervention system can be much more precise and diagnostic. The team can state that these students need additional time and support on the particular skill of solving systems of equations by substitution. This specificity provides for the targeted instruction essential to good intervention.

Should administrators view common assessment data?

Yes. If a school leader is to provide teams with the support and resources they need in order to succeed, that leader must be in a position to monitor the progress of teams. Evidence of student learning is one of the most important indicators of team progress, and principals should certainly have access to that information throughout the year. A principal who waits until the end of the year when state tests are administered to determine whether students are learning would not be an effective leader of the PLC process.

It is equally important, however, that principals and team members alike approach the results from common assessments with a learning orientation rather than a blame orientation. The prevailing question must be, What do these results tell us about how individually and collectively we can better meet the needs of students through improvements in our instructional strategy? If an entire team is struggling to get good results in teaching a skill or concept, the principal and team must brainstorm the causes and develop strategies to provide the team with timely and relevant professional development. If leaders use the results to criticize individuals or embarrass teachers, then teachers will understandably look for ways to circumvent the process.

Our district already has created common assessments, so shouldn't teacher teams just use them?

The development of common assessments by collaborative teams is simply too important to delegate entirely to the district office. In fact, we believe that team-developed common assessments are such a powerful tool in school improvement that leaders should allow no team of teachers to opt out of creating them.

The process of developing common assessments promotes regular, job-embedded staff development as part of the collaborative team process by clarifying curriculum, instructional strategies, and intervention plans; creating opportunities for teachers to sharpen their pedagogy and deepen their content knowledge; and enhancing communication among teachers about student learning.

Developing common assessments as a team at the school site also ensures that assessments are aligned with the learning targets and essential standards that the team identified as most important for its members to teach and students to learn. Finally, when teams create common assessments and share transparent results, they foster a *professional discourse* regarding which instructional practices are most effective based on actual evidence of student learning. When others create the assessments, the discussion is more likely to focus on the flaws of the assessment rather than analysis of instructional practice.

Should team common assessments align to state tests?

First and foremost, common assessments are linked to the essential curriculum and should be aligned to learning targets derived from the essential standards each team has identified as part of its efforts to respond to critical question one, What do students need to know and be able to do? If students master what is most essential in the curriculum, they will perform well on state tests.

Considering Common Assessment Specifics

I am the only person who teaches my subject on campus, so how do I give common assessments?

There are several options available to you. You could create an electronic team with others who teach your subject, develop common assessments, and share your results with one another. You could create a team with other singletons on your campus and agree to assess overarching skills that cut across your subject areas. For example, a high-leverage strategy that has proven to have a positive impact on student achievement in all subject areas is nonfiction writing. You and your colleagues could create a rubric for effective writing, provide direct instruction in writing related to your different subjects, develop common assessments, and study results together. Other skills that cut across disciplines are those listed by the Partnership for 21st Century

Learning (n.d.), such as problem solving, critical thinking, and working in collaborative groups. You and your colleagues could create projects in your various classes that require students to demonstrate these skills and a common rubric for assessing them.

Finally, you could integrate questions into your assessments for your specific content from released sets of test items from various state and national assessments. This will provide you with a basis of comparison to see how your students are performing compared to students in other states or across the country. For example, if you visit the National Center for Education Statistics website (http://nces.ed.gov/nationsreportcard), you have access to hundreds of questions that have been administered on the National Assessment of Educational Progress (n.d.) for elementary, middle, and high school students. You can use these items to assess your students on skills you are teaching and see how your students perform compared to this national sample.

We track students by ability. How can teachers compare results on common assessments when our classes vary so much?

Common assessments, by definition, assess students in the same curriculum who are expected to acquire the same knowledge and skills, using the same assessment administered at the same time. Therefore, it would serve no purpose to assess students in different tracks, with different curricula, with different intended outcomes using the same assessment.

The larger question is this: Why are you tracking students when there is abundant evidence that this practice is detrimental, particularly to those assigned to the low track, and conveys low expectations? For example, in Rick's former high school, Adlai E. Stevenson, the school offered three levels of classes. They were as follows.

1. **Honors (college level):** This series of courses prepared students for success in the advanced placement program. It gave students access to college-level courses while in high school.

2. **Regular (college preparatory):** This series of courses prepared students for success in college but did not give them access to college-level courses. The goal was to ensure students would succeed in their coursework at the university without the need for remedial courses.

3. **Accelerated:** This series of courses was offered only in the freshman and sophomore years for students who were reading far below grade level and could not be expected to succeed at the college preparatory level. The goal was very specific: to accelerate student learning by providing them with a double block of English and tutorial time so that by the time they were juniors, they could move into and succeed in the college preparatory

program. The objective was not to serve as a four-year remedial program, but rather to serve as a two-year launching pad because, as juniors, the lowest-level course available was college preparatory. The staff recognized that not all students would elect to go to college, but they believed that those who would not still needed to be able to read text closely, write persuasively, and so on.

The school recommended placement to students based on subject-specific placement exams. Any student, however, could elect to attempt a higher level. The school encouraged any student who wanted to enroll in nonsequential advanced placement courses to do so. Adlai E. Stevenson High School staff members viewed themselves as providing a bridge of support to challenging curriculum rather than as a barrier to deny students access to that curriculum.

So if you are going to have multiple levels, you must start with a clearly defined purpose for each level. Furthermore, you *must* design the lowest level to accelerate student learning so that those students move as quickly as possible to grade-level curriculum. Absent this plan to accelerate student learning, you simply create a remedial track that widens the achievement gap.

The bottom line is that *every* student who enrolls in your school is entitled to be prepared for success on high-stakes tests and should have the knowledge and skills to pursue some form of education beyond high school. There must be a rigorous baseline of proficiency for all students; however, students in advanced curriculum should be expected to achieve well beyond that baseline because otherwise there is no justification for creating a higher level.

Aren't our district benchmark tests common formative assessments? Can we use them for our team's common assessments?

Team-developed common formative assessments and district benchmark assessments typically serve different purposes. Certainly both are common. They vary, however, in terms of focus, frequency, length, and how results are used.

Common assessments designed by teams of teachers at the building level provide the greatest leverage to teacher teams because they link so closely to what they have taught in the classroom and generate timely results that allow them to immediately adjust the sequence of instruction. Ideally, they are aligned with and focused on a limited number of learning targets and are administered frequently. Most important, they target the learning needs of individual students and call for immediate intervention on specific skills taught in short-term units.

District benchmarks, whether developed by groups of teachers representing a particular department or grade level or purchased from a vendor, are administered less frequently, address many more skills and concepts, and primarily provide information on district performance rather than support for individual students. Benchmarks can help district leaders identify an area of the curriculum in which students consistently struggle across grade levels, a grade level where achievement lags behind, schools in trouble and in need of support, or schools that could serve as exemplars. This information can be very helpful, and we are not suggesting there is no place for district benchmarks. In fact, schools should be using district benchmarks in a more formative way than what they have traditionally done in the past. A school can use district benchmarks as another indicator of student proficiency and provide the appropriate level of intervention or enrichment based on the results. If an individual teacher seems to be particularly effective in helping students achieve at high levels on the benchmarks, the team could explore the strategies leading to those results. We are simply saying that district benchmarks should not be used to *replace* team-developed common formative assessments.

Does the entire assessment need to be the same to be a common assessment?

By definition, a common assessment is the same assessment for all students. Common assessments are not sort of common, mostly common, or predominantly common. A common assessment is just as the name implies—*common*—meaning teachers administer the same assessment to all students enrolled in the same class, course, or grade level at approximately the same time during the year.

Do common assessments have to be the exact same test, or can individual teachers use different assessments that align to the same rubric or proficiency criteria?

Common assessments reflect what teams expect their students to learn. They help monitor how well students are learning concepts that teams agreed were part of the essential curriculum. Data are meaningful when teacher teams talk about how their students did compared to others on the same measure, against an agreed-on standard of achievement. If assessments are not uniform and team members use different strategies for assessing students or different criteria to measure proficiency, the opportunity for meaningful comparison of student progress and performance is diminished.

Monitoring Learning

Comparing common assessment data can be uncomfortable. Are there ways to make the process less threatening?

One important step to relieve some of the anxiety associated with comparing assessment data is for the administration to assure teachers that it will not use the results from team-developed common formative assessments in the teacher evaluation process or to rank or rate teachers. Both the team and the school must approach poor student performance on a common formative assessment with a learning orientation rather than a blame orientation. The question that drives the work of the team must be, How can we help a colleague improve the learning of his or her students? rather than, Whose head must roll? The administration should only address poor performance on common formative assessments if a teacher demonstrates a persistent unwillingness to change his or her practice.

Using common assessments to rank and rate teachers is an exercise in futility. If four wonderful teachers give the same assessment, one is destined to be fourth in terms of student achievement. The fact says nothing about the quality of the teacher. On the other hand, if four of the most inept teachers to ever enter a classroom give a common assessment, one of them is certain to get the best of the terrible results. Common assessments are powerful instruments for giving teachers the information they need to improve. They are worthless as a tool for ranking or rating teachers.

Another step in relieving anxiety is to use a protocol that focuses on the practice, not the person. The conversation during data analysis is less, "Wow, Mike. You do a wonderful job of teaching this standard," and more, "Mike, what were the practices you used to get such great results on that standard?"

There is almost certain to be some initial anxiety when teams begin collectively analyzing evidence of student learning, just as there is some anxiety with any new practice. But as educators begin to engage in the process, recognize its benefits, and realize that they are not castigated if their students struggle on an assessment, that anxiety dissipates.

Should teams use a protocol when reviewing common assessment data? Where can we find examples?

We addressed the use of protocols in chapter 2 (pages 65–68), but to reiterate, protocols make team data analysis more efficient and effective, faster, and more accurate. There is no single protocol that is better than the rest for analyzing data, and teams often find it useful to try several different protocols before choosing the one that works best for them. Examples of different protocols for analyzing data can be found on the

National School Reform Faculty website (www.nsrfharmony.org/free-resources) and on AllThingsPLC (www.allthingsplc.info/files/uploads/data_analysis_protocol.pdf).

How many questions should a common assessment have?

The length of an assessment depends on the purpose and the number of targets that teachers are assessing. An assessment covering two or three targets using four or five well-written items per learning target generates more information about the learner than an assessment covering eight to ten essential standards using one or two questions per standard. Smaller chunks generate deeper understanding of the learning, catch potential problems earlier, and focus the interventions.

How many questions should we use to measure each learning target?

When using a selected-response assessment, you should generate at least four to five selected-response items for each learning target. If you use constructed-response items, one or two high-quality items may be sufficient. Teams must also establish the level of proficiency they seek. For example, if an assessment uses selected-response items and the proficiency target is 75 percent, then four high-quality items will work well. If the target for proficiency is 80 percent, then the team should consider using at least five items per learning target.

Monitoring Learning

How many learning targets should we assess on a common assessment?

We recommend between eight and ten essential standards per subject, per semester. There is no magic number in terms of how many standards or targets teams should consider on a single assessment. Using a common assessment to address a single learning target is legitimate and even desirable. More frequent common assessments over fewer learning targets are more likely to generate the most focused evidence of student learning.

An assessment that includes several standards or targets can also work but warrants a word of caution. For example, an assessment may gather evidence on four different learning targets. A student who does well on three of the four may meet the standard for the overall assessment if the team considers it as a whole, even though that student lacks proficiency in a vital skill. Remember that when it comes to monitoring student learning, the rule is "by the student and by the standard." So when using an assessment with multiple standards or learning targets, be certain to monitor each student's proficiency on each target.

What format should a team use for common assessments?

One of the biggest problems in teacher-made assessments is that the assessments do not align with what teachers say are the intended outcomes. Consider the teacher who asserts that the most essential outcome of a unit on the Civil War is that students understand the racial and regional conflicts that led to the war and have persisted since its conclusion. If the assessment for that unit relies solely on multiple-choice and true/false questions on leading generals, important battles, and the dates of significant events, the assessment reveals nothing about what the team claimed was essential student learning.

The format of the assessment should reflect the essential learning the team is targeting and provide the most helpful information about each student's proficiency. For example, if a team wants each student to be able to write to a central theme, the best assessment is to have students write rather than take a multiple-choice test. If a team wants students to be able to identify the main idea of a reading passage, a selected-response or constructed-response assessment could be most appropriate.

Furthermore, if teachers and principals are to succeed, they need information about student learning from a variety of sources. Relying on any one type, method, model, or format of assessment would be a seriously flawed assessment strategy. Assessment of a student's work should provide a rich array of information on his or her progress and achievement. The challenge is to match appropriate assessment strategies to curricular goals and instructional methodologies.

Which are better—selected-response or constructed-response items?

Once again, the appropriateness of the type of assessment to use depends on what teams are assessing. If a team seeks evidence that students can recall factual information, a selected-response assessment is perfectly appropriate. A well-constructed selected-response item can even help identify common errors in student thinking. A team attempting to gather evidence of higher-order skills will be better served by constructed-response items that call for students to explain, compare, contrast, evaluate, and so on. So it's not the item type that's most important; rather, it's the match between the type of item and the type of learning being measured that matters.

Does a common assessment only assess essential standards, or can it also assess other required curriculum?

The purpose of a common assessment is to provide teachers with useful information about a student's current level of mastery of those standards the team has identified as *essential*. That should always be the priority. If the team has the time to assess other curriculum as well, leaders should not prevent it from doing so. While teachers will likely teach more than they test, common assessments should reflect what team members have agreed matters most.

Can we use the same assessment to retest after interventions?

Teams can be more confident of student proficiency after intervention if they administer a different assessment that focuses on the same skills rather than reusing the same assessment.

Do we have to give common assessments at the same time? Does there need to be a common pacing guide?

A common assessment is used to assess the learning of students in the same curriculum who are expected to acquire the same knowledge and skills through the use of the same instrument or the same criteria, and teachers should administer these assessments at the same time or within a very narrow window of opportunity. Therefore, the team does need to establish a common pacing guide. This pacing guide does not dictate that students must be on a certain page on a certain date, but it does establish the timeline for a unit of instruction. Day-to-day pacing may vary from teacher to teacher, but the entire team knows that on a certain date, direct instruction will stop as the team administers its common assessment. The assessment is no longer common if one teacher takes three weeks for a unit and another takes six weeks. Furthermore, without common pacing, it is impossible for a team to provide students with equal access to a guaranteed and viable curriculum. In a PLC, pacing is no longer the decision of each teacher but instead becomes the purview of the entire team.

What are the keys to high-quality, performance-based assessments?

High-quality, performance-based assessments require team members to address two challenges. First, do team members agree on the criteria by which they will judge the quality of student work? Answering this question requires a high degree of specificity.

A team can agree that it wants all students to be able to write a good persuasive essay, but that agreement is irrelevant if members can't agree on the specific elements that constitute a good persuasive essay. Second, teams must be able to apply the agreed-on criteria with the consistency necessary to establish inter-rater reliability. This means the rubrics the team creates provide specificity that allows team members to give students consistent feedback on their work. Furthermore, the rubrics should help students assess the quality of their own work. The only way teams can reach this level of proficiency on performance-based assessments is to practice applying their rubrics to examples of student work month after month until variations in scoring are eliminated.

Doesn't the fixation on assessment ignore the importance of the whole child?

Schools are particularly prone to the "Tyranny of Or" (Collins & Porras, 1997). Educators often assume they must choose between strong administrators or autonomous teachers, phonics or whole language, emphasis on core curriculum or commitment to the arts, leadership anchored in the central office or site-based management, and so on. One of the most damaging examples of the Tyranny of Or is the belief that a focus on academics leads to indifference on all the other factors that constitute the well-being of a student. Thomas Lickona (2004), director of the Center for Respect and Responsibility and noted author on character education, calls for educators to create "schools of character," which he describes as:

> A community of virtue, a place where moral and intellectual qualities such as good judgment, best effort, respect, kindness, honesty, service, and citizenship are modeled, upheld, celebrated, and practiced in every part of the school's life—from the examples of the adults to the relationship among peers, the handling of discipline, the content of the curriculum, the rigor of academic standards, the ethos of the environment, the conduct of extracurricular activities, and the involvement of parents. (p. 219)

Lickona recommends three resources to help educators create such schools, and *Professional Learning Communities at Work: Best Practices for Enhancing Student Achievement* (DuFour & Eaker, 1998) is one of those resources. Clearly, he does not believe that a PLC's commitment to the academic achievement of students interferes with the development of the whole child.

Those who contend schools must focus on either academic achievement or the well-being of students are presenting a false dichotomy. They should let go of the Tyranny of Or.

Does attention to a guaranteed curriculum, common pacing, and common assessments come at the cost of teacher creativity?

No. Keep in mind that each teacher is free to use the instructional strategies he or she believes will help students acquire the most essential skills and concepts. Also keep in mind that teachers working in teams have the key role in determining those essential skills and concepts and how to assess them. The team can be very creative in how it chooses to assess students. Bringing people together in a collaborative endeavor fosters greater creativity than an environment in which people work in isolation.

Understanding the District's Role

Does district leadership need to answer the question, How will we know when our students have learned it? If so, what information should they gather?

Absolutely. Once again, if district leaders wait until the end of the year to discover whether students have learned when state tests are administered, they are in no position to support students and schools that may need help.

District-level assessments typically serve a different purpose from those administered by the collaborative team at the end of the unit. The team assessment identifies students who need intervention or extended learning, by name and by need, in order to provide those students with *immediate* support. District assessments are intended to gather more general information about student achievement. Is there an area of the curriculum where student performance lags behind other areas? Is there a grade level in which students consistently experience difficulty in meeting standards? Is there a subset of students not succeeding in our schools? Are there schools in trouble? Are there schools that are getting fantastic results that could serve as models for other schools in the district? Districts that administer benchmark assessments on agreed-on essential skills two or three times per year are in a better position to address these questions and provide the kind of support that educators need to succeed in what they are being asked to do. District assessments should, however, never replace team-developed common formative assessments, which serve as the linchpin of the PLC process.

Monitoring Learning

What is the district's role in supporting the use of common assessments?

In order for teachers to maximize the impact of data from common assessments, districts should ensure that data:

- Are easily accessible

- Are purposefully arranged

- Lead to focused dialogue regarding student learning and effective instruction

In districts where making meaning of assessment data is a powerful experience, the district takes responsibility for developing the necessary structures associated with the first two prerequisites and creating the conditions essential to the third.

Teachers' access to the data must be timely. Data lose their impact whenever it takes more than forty-eight hours to return the results of a common assessment to teachers. Outdated information makes it more difficult for teachers to adjust instruction, identify students who need more time and support, or coordinate intervention or enrichment programs. To improve the accessibility of data, the district needs to create systems that shorten the turnaround time for reporting data.

The data must also be purposefully arranged—that is, administrators present them to teacher teams in a format that is complete, accurate, and straightforward. Data should be organized in simple—not simplistic—ways. There are many software packages that quickly, almost instantaneously, provide assessment results in tables, charts, or graphs and make it easy for teachers to digest the results of interim assessments. From time to time, teachers may create their own tables or graphs or request additional formats for organizing assessment results, but they should receive the initial data arranged in a way that allows them to focus on the results—not the presentation format.

Even if data are easily accessible and purposefully arranged, they will not impact student learning unless educators engage together in focused, intentional discussion of assessment results. Reflective teaching is most powerful when it is collective rather than isolated and when it is based on actual evidence of student learning. Without this team dialogue and the resulting actions based on the discussion, common formative assessments will not contribute to improved performance for students or educators.

How can the district ensure that teams have access to the right kind of data at the right time?

The first two of the three conditions described in the previous question—making data easily accessible and purposefully arranging them—are administrative responsibilities. Having structures such as the hardware, software, training, and procedures in place is a necessary but insufficient condition to ensure teams use data effectively. The presence of these structures alone does not ensure teams will analyze data, adjust instruction, and provide more time and support for students, but the absence of such structures almost guarantees that this won't happen.

Time is precious in schools, and with so many sophisticated software packages and data-management systems available, there may be no greater waste of time and talent than having teachers and administrators spend their valuable time manually loading data into Excel spreadsheets. Making certain that the structures are in place so that data are easily accessible and purposefully arranged is the best way for districts to ensure that teams have access to the right kind of data at the right time.

Additional PLC Resources to Dig Deeper: How Will We Know When Our Students Have Learned It?

- Bailey, K., & Jakicic, C. (2012). *Common formative assessment: A toolkit for Professional Learning Communities at Work*. Bloomington, IN: Solution Tree Press.

- Erkens, C. (2016). *Collaborative common assessments: Teamwork. Instruction. Results.* Bloomington, IN: Solution Tree Press.

- Reeves, D. (Ed.). (2007). *Ahead of the curve: The power of assessment to transform teaching and learning*. Bloomington, IN: Solution Tree Press.

- Wiliam, D. (2011). *Embedded formative assessment*. Bloomington, IN: Solution Tree Press.

Final Thoughts

Until educators are using evidence of student learning generated from team-developed common formative assessments to inform and improve their individual and collective practice, they are not fully engaged in the PLC process. This collective analysis to better meet the individual needs of students and to improve instructional practice represents the very heart of the PLC process.

Monitoring Learning

Chapter 5

How Will We Respond When Some Students Don't Learn and When Some Do?

How a school responds when students don't learn is where the rubber hits the road in the PLC process. A school can do everything described in the previous chapters of this book, including:

- Build consensus on its mission, vision, values, and goals

- Dedicate weekly collaboration time

- Form the right teams

- Identify essential learning outcomes

- Create and administer common assessments

- Identify students who have not mastered essential standards after core instruction

But at this point, if the school does not effectively help the students who are not learning at high levels, and extend the learning for the ones who are, then what has it truly achieved? The same students failing before the team started collaborating are probably still failing—the only difference is the teachers now fail these students as a team instead of individually.

Like all the elements of the PLC process, we are tight on the school's systematic and collective response when students don't learn but loose on *how* each school responds. The specific steps a school takes to intervene for struggling students will likely look different at an elementary school than at a high school, and different at a school that serves a large number of at-risk youth in comparison to a school where a majority of entering students have already mastered prerequisite skills and knowledge. Nevertheless, there are frequent, common questions we receive from PLC schools at all levels regarding how to best respond when students don't learn. In this chapter, we share research-based answers that can help accelerate your school's success on the PLC journey.

Defining Intervention

What is an intervention?

An *intervention* is anything a school does, above and beyond what all students receive, that helps certain students succeed in school (Buffum et al., 2012). If all students receive a particular instructional practice or service, it is part of the school's core instructional program. But if the school provides a specific practice, program, or service to some students, it is an intervention. Interventions are not just for academics or for remediation. Behavior, attendance, and health services can be interventions, as can enrichment for students who have already mastered grade-level essential standards.

What are systematic interventions?

Interventions are systematic when a school can make the following promise to every student: *It does not matter which teacher or teachers you are assigned to in this school. If you need additional time and support to learn at high levels, we guarantee you will receive it* (Buffum et al., 2012). To achieve this outcome, a school must build a culture of collective responsibility for student success. In such a culture, teachers do not view students as "my students and your students," "my class and your class," "special education and regular education," or "ELs and English speakers." Instead, all students are *our* students. Also, the school must have a timely, systematic process to identify students for additional support.

What are the characteristics of effective interventions?

For an intervention to be effective, it must align to *all* the following characteristics.

- **Systematic:** An intervention is systematic when the school can guarantee that every student who needs a specific intervention receives it. This requires the school to have a systematic way to identify every student who needs the intervention, regardless of what teacher he or she is assigned to for core instruction. The school also has to create a master schedule in which every student can receive the help—during the school day—without missing new instruction on essential standards. Finally, the school needs to allocate the resources and staff to meet the needs of all the identified students.

- **Research based:** There must be research showing that the intervention has a high likelihood of working, or evidence that the intervention is working for a vast majority of students currently in the intervention. In a perfect world, a specific intervention would meet both criteria.

- **Targeted:** Interventions are most effective when targeted by student and by standard. This is why answering PLC critical question one is so important to effective interventions. When a school fails to get focused on exactly what students must learn, it ends up using broad indicators to identify and group students for intervention—such as report card grades, universal screening results, district benchmark tests, and state assessments. These assessments measure multiple learning targets, so students might score below proficient for multiple reasons. As a result, the educators responsible for leading the intervention cannot target instruction for the intervention because the students identified share the same symptom (failing the test or class) but not the same cause.

- **Timely:** Teachers should not allow students to struggle too long before assisting them. The longer students are allowed to fail, the deeper the academic hole they dig, and the harder it will be to get them out. A school should have a systematic process to identify students for interventions at least every three weeks.

- **Administered by a trained professional:** The effectiveness of any intervention is directly linked to the competency and expertise of the adult leading it. As a general rule, the greater the need of the students in the intervention, the greater the need for an expert interventionist in the targeted area of need.

- **Directive:** Students must be required to attend in the same monitored and timely fashion that student attendance is required and monitored in regular classroom instruction. When interventions are optional, usually the only students who take advantage of the support are those already succeeding, and the last students to attend are the most at risk and in dire need of support. If a school claims its mission is to ensure all students learn at high levels, it cannot allow some students to choose to fail.

When a specific intervention aligns to all these traits, it will be highly effective at meeting the targeted outcomes.

What is response to intervention (RTI)? How does it fit into PLCs and interventions?

Response to intervention (RTI) is a systematic process of tiered support to ensure every student receives the additional time and support needed to learn at high levels. A multitiered system of support (MTSS), RTI's underlying premise is that schools should not delay providing help for struggling students until they fall far enough behind to qualify for special education, but instead should provide timely, targeted,

Ensuring Learning

systematic interventions to all students who demonstrate the need (Buffum et al., 2012). The research and evidence supporting RTI practices is comprehensive and compelling. In perhaps the most extensive study of the factors that impact student learning, John Hattie (2012) found that RTI ranks second in the most effective influences, inside or outside of school, that can increase student performance.

PLC and RTI are both processes focused on the same outcome: improved student learning. They are grounded in a common base of research, and many of the defining practices are identical. Where the processes are not the same, they are perfectly complementary. PLCs focus on a learning-centered school culture and the collaborative structures necessary to achieve the goal of improved student learning. While PLCs address the need to collectively respond when students don't learn, they do not specifically describe the steps needed to create a system of interventions. Therefore, individual schools that embraced the PLC process before the days of RTI created their own systems and processes for intervention through trial and error. Fortunately, RTI provides more specifics on how to create a tiered process of academic interventions, which would prove most helpful to schools functioning as PLCs in their efforts to answer the question, How will we respond when some students don't learn? Likewise, RTI requires a learning-centered school culture and collaborative structures to be effective. While RTI does not specifically describe how to do this, PLCs do.

Finding Time for Intervention

We lack the staffing we need to effectively provide interventions. What do we do?

Most schools feel they do not have enough time, adequate staff, sufficient resources, or small-enough class sizes to meet the needs of all their students. We find this to be the case at schools regardless if the average class size is thirty-five or twenty or if the school has twelve instructional aides on staff or two. Our point is that for every school that says it can't provide interventions because it doesn't have the resources, there are similar schools doing it with less. For example, figure 5.1 was the pyramid of interventions for Pioneer Middle School in Southern California when Mike Mattos was principal until 2009. California public schools consistently rank near the bottom nationally in per-pupil spending. Following are the average class sizes and support staff available at the school to provide all the services listed on its pyramid, meeting the needs of its approximately 1,500 students.

- **Average class size:** Thirty-four students per class in core subjects, fifty-five in physical education, and sixty in fine arts
- **Administration:** One principal and one assistant principal

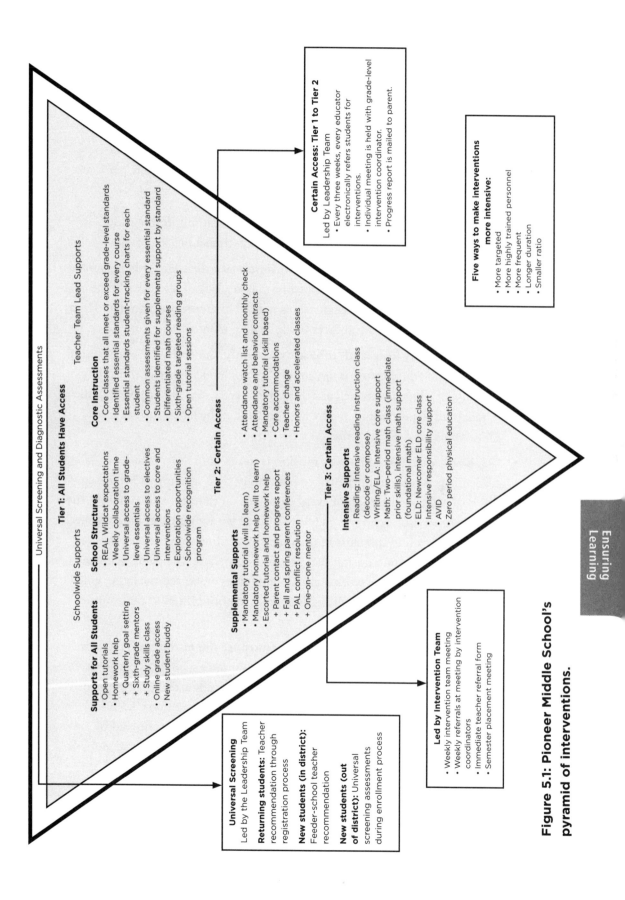

Figure 5.1: Pioneer Middle School's pyramid of interventions.

Universal Screening and Diagnostic Assessments

Tier 1: All Students Have Access

Schoolwide Supports   Teacher Team Lead Supports

Supports for All Students
- Open tutorials
- Homework help
+ Quarterly goal setting
+ Sixth-grade mentors
- Study skills class
- Online grade access
- New student buddy

School Structures
- REAL Wildcat expectations
- Weekly collaboration time
- Universal access to grade-level essentials
- Universal access to electives
- Universal access to core and interventions
- Exploration opportunities
- Schoolwide recognition program

Core Instruction
- Core classes that all meet or exceed grade-level standards
- Identified essential standards for every course
- Essential standards student-tracking charts for each student
- Common assessments given for every essential standard
- Students identified for supplemental support by standard
- Differentiated math courses
- Sixth-grade targeted reading groups
- Open tutorial sessions

Tier 2: Certain Access

Supplemental Supports
- Mandatory tutorial (will to learn)
- Mandatory homework help (will to learn)
- Escorted tutorial and homework help
+ Parent contact and progress report
+ Fall and spring parent conferences
+ PAL conflict resolution
+ One-on-one mentor

- Attendance watch list and monthly check
- Attendance and behavior contracts
- Mandatory tutorial (skill based)
- Core accommodations
- Teacher change
- Honors and accelerated classes

Tier 3: Certain Access

Intensive Supports
- Reading: Intensive reading instruction class (decode or compose)
- Writing/ELA: Intensive core support
- Math: Two-period math class (immediate prior skills), intensive math support (foundational math)
- ELD: Newcomer ELD core class
- Intensive responsibility support
- AVID
- Zero period physical education

Certain Access: Tier 1 to Tier 2
Led by Leadership Team
- Every three weeks, every educator electronically refers students for interventions.
- Individual meeting is held with grade-level intervention coordinator.
- Progress report is mailed to parent.

Five ways to make interventions more intensive:
- More targeted
- More highly trained personnel
- More frequent
- Longer duration
- Smaller ratio

Universal Screening
Led by the Leadership Team

Returning students: Teacher recommendation through registration process

New students (in district): Feeder-school teacher recommendation

New students (out of district): Universal screening assessments during enrollment process

Led by Intervention Team
- Weekly intervention team meeting
- Weekly referrals at meeting by intervention coordinators
- Immediate teacher referral form
- Semester placement meeting

Ensuring Learning

- **Counseling:** One counselor
- **Special education:** Two special education teachers
- **Instructional aides:** Three part-time aides (two for special education and one for English learners)
- **School psychologist, speech/language pathologist, and nurse:** District staff serving the needs of several schools and on site only one day per week
- **Librarian:** One part-time media aide (no librarian)
- **Classified staff:** Two and a half office secretary positions, four custodians, one full-time campus supervisor, and two part-time lunch supervisors

We have found there are many schools that have twice the staff for half as many students that claim interventions are impossible due to a lack of resources. To be able to provide all the interventions and extensions needed to ensure every student learns at high levels, the Pioneer staff embraces the following mantras.

- **"There is no 'my kids' and 'your kids' . . . only 'our kids.'"** Pioneer found that they were duplicating interventions for students in special education and regular education as well as across grade levels. Whenever possible, the school tried to group students by need, instead of by labels such as *special education*, *Title I*, *EL*, or *grade status*.

- **"All hands on deck."** Pioneer's mission is to maximize every student's academic potential and personal responsibility. This means that achieving this goal is the primary job of every employee on campus. Subsequently, the campus supervisor (who was a college student working to become a teacher) assisted the reading specialist in the intensive reading support class and ran an intervention group during the intervention period. The plant foreman supervised the privilege work area. All employees embraced the larger goal of the school, instead of limiting their daily responsibilities to the confines of their specific job descriptions.

- **"Stop doing what isn't working and repurpose the resources."** Pioneer had many traditional interventions (such as summer school, a special education directed studies class, and mandatory study halls) that were not showing results. The same students were in these interventions day after day and year after year, with little evidence of improvement. Instead of continuing to allocate resources to these failed interventions, the school decided to reallocate and repurpose the staff to efforts that could lead to better results.

- **"The more targeted the intervention, the more likely it will work."** Pioneer had too many different student needs in the same intervention, which divided the focus and impact of the assigned staff. To counter this, the staff became obsessed with the question, What exactly do we want students to be able to know and do in this intervention? The more clearly the staff and students knew exactly what the goal of the intervention was, the more quickly students achieved the outcome and were dismissed from the intervention, thus saving time and resources.

We are not suggesting that limited resources are not a difficulty when creating a system of interventions. But in most cases, this reality should be a hurdle to overcome with creative and targeted thinking, not an insurmountable obstacle used to justify maintaining the status quo.

We do not have time in our schedule for interventions, so what do we do?

Even the most effective core instruction will not successfully meet the needs of every student. Every time teachers introduce a new essential standard, a learning-focused school must anticipate that some students will not master it by the end of the unit. When a majority of students are successful, classroom teachers must move on to the next unit of study. But for students who have not mastered the previous unit's essential standards, the school will need to provide time for additional support on these standards, without those students missing new initial core instruction.

Considering these facts, the question a learning-focused school must ask is not, "*Should* we create intervention time during the school day?" but instead, "*How* will we create supplemental and intensive intervention time during our school day?" Hundreds of schools throughout North America and beyond have successfully revised their master schedules to create intervention time without lengthening the school day, and within existing state guidelines, contractual agreements, and site resources. We recommend that a school create a task force, which includes teacher leaders and administration, and study what similar schools are doing. The website www.allthingsPLC.info features hundreds of model PLC schools. Each of these schools has dedicated time, during the school day, in which students can receive additional time and support without missing new essential direct instruction. Also, the anthologies *It's About Time: Planning Interventions and Extensions in Elementary School* (Buffum & Mattos, 2015) and *It's About Time: Planning Interventions and Extensions in Secondary School* (Mattos & Buffum, 2015) feature chapters from model schools both about how they created the time and also how they used the time.

Ensuring Learning

How much time should a school dedicate weekly to supplemental interventions?

The primary purpose of supplemental interventions, which the response to intervention (RTI) process calls Tier 2 interventions, is to provide students extra time and support to meet essential academic and behavior standards. When building time into a school schedule, we recommend the following criteria.

- The school's master schedule should dedicate time *at least* twice a week for supplemental interventions. At schools with larger numbers of at-risk youth, every day might be necessary.

- Each session should be around thirty minutes long. When the goal is to reteach a specific standard, about thirty minutes is a sufficient amount of time for most educators to teach a targeted, direct lesson. Dedicating time for interventions does come at a cost, as the school is really taking time traditionally used to solely introduce new curriculum and instead using it for the reteaching of essential standards. So a school wants to allocate as much as necessary but not more.

- Time must be available to all students. Supplemental intervention time must be during the school day, preferably during a dedicated instructional period. Many schools try to find this time by extending the school day for interventions, offering extra help before school, at lunch, during recess, and after school. Unfortunately, these options have unavoidable drawbacks. Most schools cannot require a student to come early or stay late, especially if the student depends on school transportation, must work to support his or her family, or is needed at home to tend to younger siblings. Also, before- and after-school and lunchtime interventions usually extend beyond teachers' contracted student-contact time. This means that the staff best trained to reteach essential standards—teachers—are not available to help. When the schedule embeds intervention time in the school day, teachers are available to help, and all students must attend.

- Students cannot miss new essential standards. Teachers should never introduce new essential standards during supplemental intervention time. It is acceptable to introduce new content to students who do not need interventions as long as the content has not been identified by the team as essential.

Within these four criteria, there should be flexibility for each school to create an intervention schedule that best meets the needs of their students and staff, and within the specific contractual agreements of the district.

Where can we find sample schedules?

The website www.allthingsPLC.info features hundreds of model PLC schools. Each of these schools has dedicated time, during the school day, in which students can receive additional time and support without missing new essential direct instruction.

There are also master schedules provided at the following links.

- **Elementary examples:** www.allthingsplc.info/files/uploads/schedule _examples_elementary.pdf

- **Middle and high school examples:** www.allthingsplc.info/files/uploads /middle_high_intervention_examples.pdf

- **Database of PLC schools:** www.allthingsplc.info/evidence

Also, the anthologies *It's About Time: Planning Interventions and Extensions in Elementary School* (Buffum & Mattos, 2015) and *It's About Time: Planning Interventions and Extensions in Secondary School* (Mattos & Buffum, 2015) feature chapters from model schools both about how they created the time and also how they used the time.

How do we provide interventions for students who are years behind in foundational skills?

There are six universal skills of learning—skills that span all subjects and grade levels. They are:

1. Reading

2. Writing

3. Number sense

4. English language or school or primary language

5. Regular attendance

6. Appropriate social and academic behaviors

If a student is significantly weak or multiple years below grade level in any one of these areas, he or she will struggle in every subject and in every year in school until educators adequately address the deficiency.

The keys to effective intensive interventions are as follows.

- The interventions must be part of the student's daily schedule.

- The student must still have access to essential grade-level curriculum.

- Highly trained professionals in the student's area of need must provide or guide the interventions.

- The interventions must target the cause of the student's struggles, not just the symptoms.

To diagnose the needs and determine the most effective interventions for each student in need of intensive interventions, we recommend that the school creates a site intervention team.

If some students need a lot of additional time to catch up, then shouldn't retention be an option as an intensive intervention?

The research on the effectiveness of retention is abundant and conclusive—retention does not promote higher levels of learning, close achievement gaps, or increase an at-risk student's odds of future success in school. The most comprehensive meta-analysis on retention found that being retained one year almost doubled a student's likelihood of dropping out, while being retained twice almost guaranteed it (Hattie, 2009). There are also significant equity concerns regarding the use of retention. A comprehensive study from the Office of Civil Rights found that retention rates are highest among traditionally disadvantaged minorities (West, 2012). For any school dedicated to ensuring that all students learn at high levels, retention should not be an option.

We have too much content to cover. How can we stop to provide interventions?

We understand the concern expressed in this question, but we challenge the logic. Think about it: A PLC is dedicated to a mission of ensuring that all students learn at high levels. To achieve this outcome, teacher teams have identified the absolutely essential learning outcomes, unit by unit, that all students must master to be prepared and successful in the next unit, grade level, or course. The school also knows that no matter how effectively teachers initially explain each essential standard, some students will not master these critical learning outcomes by the end of the unit. So when it comes to providing these students extra time and support, would a learning-focused school decide it is more important for teachers to introduce additional nonessential curriculum or to dedicate time for students to receive additional help and extension on the most important curriculum? The answer to this question is clear to a school dedicated to learning, not teaching.

We suspect that some educators would argue that schools don't have the power to make this decision, as the state, province, or district has dictated that the entire curriculum must be covered. In reality, teachers are making this choice every day in their individual classrooms. There is hardly a teacher in the United States who can prove he or she is teaching every standard and learning target dictated by others, as there is just too much to cover. So, in classrooms all over North America every day, teachers prioritize the curriculum, adjust unit plans, and fail to cover the entire intended curriculum by the end of the year. If individual teachers can do it, then why can't teams of teachers?

Specifying Roles

What is the parent's responsibility for interventions?

Without question, parental support can benefit a school's intervention efforts, as well as build trust and support with the school's parental community. In chapter 1 (pages 17–18), we referenced a very specific list of commitments that the parents of Adlai E. Stevenson High School made as part of the school's vision and collective commitments process. But even when a school has created such clarity of responsibility in the school-to-home partnership, there are factors that a learning-focused school must acknowledge and address, including the following.

- Most schools cannot require parents to actually meet these expectations.

- Often the students who need interventions the most come from home environments in which the parent or guardian is unable or unwilling to provide scholastic support at home.

- Even when parents have the time and desire to help their children learn essential standards—such as solving a linear equation—it is unlikely they will have more effective ways to teach the concept than the credentialed teachers at the school.

In the end, there is only one essential task that a school can expect of parents: make sure their children attend school. The law is on our side when parents fail to meet this minimal responsibility. A school should certainly make every effort to engage parents in their children's education and request their support when their students need extra help. But there is a law of diminishing returns, where the valuable time and effort that staff members use to solicit parental support would be better spent directly helping the student at school.

What is the student's responsibility for interventions?

The student's primary responsibility, both during core instruction and interventions, is to demonstrate motivation and tenacity—the ability to give effort toward the task at hand and to stick with it until it is completed successfully. When students receive effective instruction to meet their learning needs, and apply themselves to the work, high levels of learning ensue. But here is a critical point: motivation and volition are not genetic attributes. A learning-focused school should expect that some students will lack the maturity, self-motivation, parental support, or vision to embrace the importance of school or the effort required to succeed. This is why interventions must be directive. At-risk students must not get the option to attend interventions, nor the choice of trying and sticking with them until they succeed. We can teach motivation and volition by requiring students to demonstrate them.

Who is responsible for providing interventions—classroom teachers or support staff?

Both classroom teachers and support staff are responsible for providing interventions. The key is to be clear on who should lead which interventions, for when everyone is in charge of something, no one is. Because teacher teams in the PLC process share essential learning outcomes, we recommend that each team takes lead responsibility for providing interventions in its team-specific essential content standards. Wouldn't it make sense that a third-grade team of teachers takes primary responsibility to assist students who need additional time and support in learning third-grade essential standards? And wouldn't it make sense that the high school biology team takes the lead to support students who require additional assistance in learning essential biology learning outcomes? It is likely that the students who need additional help in third-grade or biology standards will represent a spectrum of the school's demographics: regular education, special education, English learners, the economically disadvantaged, and students identified as gifted. But, regardless of student labels, the staff members most likely to be trained in these standards would be the classroom teachers in these subject areas.

Likewise, every school has additional staff to support students, such as:

- Administrators
- A counselor
- A school psychologist
- A speech and language pathologist
- Special education teachers
- A librarian
- Health services staff

- Subject specialists (a reading specialist, a mathematics specialist, and so on)

- Instructional aides

- Classified staff (secretaries, custodial staff, and supervisors)

These personnel can provide interventions based on the skill, expertise, and availability of each staff member. For example, a reading specialist or special education teacher often has a depth of expertise and experience in providing intensive remediation in foundational skills. A school counselor or school psychologist usually has training in leading social and academic behavior interventions as well as in identifying home environmental needs. When a student's need is not an academic skill problem but instead a will problem, then administration and classified staff can take the lead on requiring students to show effort and complete assigned work. These examples are not intended to be the only way to allocate staff to lead interventions. The specific staff members, as well as their training and experience, will vary from school to school.

When it comes down to allocating staff for interventions, the school should ask two critical questions: What does each student need to be able to learn at high levels? and Who on our staff is best trained and available to meet this need?

How should we use our specialist teachers for interventions?

We don't think the question, How do we best use the gifted program coordinator? is the right one to ask. Nor is, How do we best use our special education staff? Instead, the better question is, What do our students need, and who is best trained and available to meet each specific need? Applying this thinking to your current job responsibilities, the better question is, How can my skills, training, and talents best ensure that more students learn at high levels, based on the needs of the students I might serve?

How do elective teachers fit into interventions?

If elective teachers work in job-alike teams and answer the PLC critical questions for their subjects, then these teachers have essential standards that students need to learn in their subjects. Elective teachers can use supplemental intervention time to support students in their curriculum. We have visited schools in which some specialists and elective teachers have identified how their curriculum can support essential core standards in ELA, mathematics, science, and social studies. If this is the case, then these teachers could assist with supporting these core skills, as well as help students learn the essential standards of their content areas.

Ensuring Learning

How do you make students attend an intervention?

The first step in making interventions directive is to schedule intervention time during the school day. When schools offer interventions before or after school, then parental approval and school transportation can limit student attendance.

Next, you should consider this question: How does your school get students to attend their regular classes? Virtually every school has the majority of their students attend class on time every day. Does this happen because students intrinsically are driven to attend core instructional time, but lose their motivation to learn during interventions? Of course not! Students attend first period because their schools clearly expect them to. Teachers record student attendance every day and take clearly defined actions when students are absent. Teachers are not required to go find the students who are absent from their classes. The administration, counselors, and office staff support this schoolwide effort. The school has a balance of positive recognitions and privileges for proper attendance and timely consequences when students fail to meet these expectations. So how do you make students attend interventions? Do the same things your school does to get students to class the first time.

Hundreds of schools have figured out processes to monitor student attendance and progress in interventions that do not require undue amounts of staff time and paperwork. Please check the See the Evidence section of AllThingsPLC (www.allthingsplc .info/evidence) for examples.

Should interventions be punitive?

Many schools assume that a student's failure is due primarily to poor attitude and effort on his or her part, and they subsequently resort to traditionally punitive consequences to address this concern. This is equivalent to the old saying, "The beatings will continue until morale improves!" The faculty can take a more effective approach by viewing interventions as what they do *for* their students, not *to* their students. What students are required to do in an intervention might not be what a student likes or wants to do. But the student must feel the adults' motivation is not to punish him or her for failure, but instead to demonstrate that the school cares so much about the student's success in school that they will not let the student fail.

Where does special education fit into a school's system of interventions?

In a PLC, we learn together about best practice, apply what we have learned, and use evidence of student learning to guide next steps. If these are the criteria for making decisions in a PLC, then the research and evidence is clear: special education has proven to be tragically insufficient and ineffective as an intervention. The graduation rate of special education students is almost 20 percent lower than regular education students (Diament, 2014), and those students are also woefully underrepresented in postsecondary education (Samuels, 2010). At your school, are special education students excelling due to the additional support they receive? Are a majority of students closing their achievement gaps? For most schools, the answer would be a resounding, "No!" If there is no research to suggest traditional special education services are likely to be effective, and no evidence at your school that these practices work, then how can a learning-focused school continue to perpetuate these interventions?

The failure of special education as an effective learning intervention is not due to ineffective special education teachers but because the purpose of special education was a civil rights issue to allow students with disabilities to attend school at all. Subsequently, traditional special education policies have allowed at-risk students to fall too far behind before receiving systematic help, disengaged general education teachers from the intervention process, and overwhelmed special education resources at the school site with far too many students to serve (Buffum et al., 2012).

If there was no such thing as special education and regular education, how would you determine who would provide interventions and how they would do so? You would group together students with common needs and then assign teachers based on who is best trained to meet those specific needs. So start by identifying students who need help, discuss each student's needs, group students by common needs, and assign staff members according to their training to meet these needs. The federal reauthorization of special education in 2003 promotes early intervention services (EIS), which allow schools to use a percentage of special education resources in preventive ways to support students not currently in special education. And regular education teachers have always been allowed to serve special education students—that is considered the least-restrictive learning environment. Such an approach might require rewriting some students' individualized education plans (IEPs), but luckily, IEPs are not chiseled in stone.

Identifying Student Needs

How often should a school systematically identify students for interventions?

It is always easier to stop a problem when it is small, so a school should systematically identify students who need extra time and support at least every three weeks. (By *systematic*, we mean that teacher participation is not optional.) If a school waits any longer, this means some students could fail for more than a month before receiving

Ensuring Learning

help. We often ask teachers, "How far behind can a student get in your class in a month?" The response is usually, "A lot!" followed by a heavy sigh. Allow students to dig themselves into a deep hole at school, and it might become their academic grave.

What do we do with students who have already learned it while some students receive interventions?

If a school schedules flexible time in the master schedule to provide students with interventions, there is no reason why teachers cannot also use this time to extend the learning of those students who have already learned it. This time can be used as follows.

- Extend a student's learning on an essential standard from proficient to advanced. For example, a student who scored a "3—Meets Proficiency" on a four-point rubric in persuasive writing could receive additional time and support to reach a "4—Exceeds Proficiency."

- Teach the nonessential curriculum. We have stressed throughout this book that the essential standards teachers identify do not represent all the curriculum that they will teach, but instead represent the *minimum* a student must master. That means that teachers can instruct students who have already mastered the essentials on the rest of the curriculum. That is a lot of available curriculum.

Notice that we keep using the word *extension*, not *enrichment*. *Extension* means to deepen students' knowledge and skills in their core instruction. *Enrichment* is traditionally the term we use to represent special and elective subjects like art, music, computers, drama, and physical education. We highly recommend that schools do not view these subjects as nonessential content that students receive only when they have learned the essential ELA and mathematics content. Electives are essential for two reasons.

1. Electives teach universal skills, often through different modalities. If a student has difficulty in fractions, then learning three-quarters time in music can be an excellent way to teach him or her the concept where repeated abstract whiteboard problems and worksheets failed. Home economics can teach the same skills, as students double a recipe for cookies while at the same time engaging in real-life applications of mathematics.

2. Students often see enrichment and electives as the fun part of school, increasing their interest, enthusiasm, and attendance. Many schools complain that their most at-risk students are apathetic while they strip away the coursework these students might excel in and enjoy.

When schools view intervention and extension as two sides of the same coin, and use their supplemental intervention time to achieve both, it is much easier to ensure that all students receive enrichment as well.

How do we fit core instruction, interventions, extensions, specials, and electives all into a student's daily schedule?

What we have advocated in this chapter is for schools to create a master schedule in which all students have access to:

- Grade-level essential standards in their core instruction

- Additional time and support to intervene and extend learning, including additional classes and coursework if needed

- Specials and electives, such as art, drama, music, and so on

When educators ask us how to schedule all of this, the question is almost always regarding the most at-risk students and how a school can fit in all the items on the list. Our response is this: How does your school currently schedule your most advanced students? At most high schools in the United States, the school's most high-achieving students:

- Take the required coursework needed to graduate

- Take additional academic courses, such as advanced placement classes and multiple years of a foreign language

- Play a sport, which most likely requires placement in a specific physical education course for at least part of the year and often beyond the required number of years of physical education required to graduate

- Take multiple extracurricular electives, including band, drama, chorus, student government, Model United Nations, Academic Pentathlon, and so on

Surprisingly, we almost never receive questions from educators about how to make the schedule work for these students, as the school has already created multiple ways to meet their unique scheduling needs. These solutions often include offering before- and after-school class options, summer school, and independent study. In fact, we would bet that if the senior star quarterback on the high school football team was an International Baccalaureate student, and was elected student-body president, and needed to be in the football period of physical education, and still needed to take all the classes required to graduate, the administration would move the sun, moon, and stars to make the school schedule work for that student. They would not ask the student to either stay in football *or* stay in International Baccalaureate *or* be in student government *or* graduate on time.

Ensuring Learning

We are not suggesting that making the master schedule work for every student is easy, or is always possible. Our point is this: if virtually every school in North America can find creative solutions for the most advanced students—who are often in the school's most public programs and have the most demanding parents—then why can't the school make a schedule for their most at-risk students who need access to courses to graduate and to remedial support classes to make up gaps in previous learning while still keeping an elective class? If most schools use the same creative thinking and sense of urgency they apply to the star quarterback's schedule, they usually find the answer for the most at-risk students. For real-life examples of schools that have achieved these outcomes, visit the See the Evidence section of AllThingsPLC (www.allthingsplc. info/evidence).

Some teachers say they know their students best, and they differentiate in their own classrooms. Is this an effective way to provide interventions?

We know that there is no way an individual teacher has all the skills, knowledge, and professional time necessary to meet the diverse needs of all the students assigned to his or her classroom. Schools can only meet these diverse student needs when the staff leverages their collective knowledge and skills.

Our state test scores are outstanding, and most of our students are succeeding. Do we really need to make so many changes for such a small number of students?

First, mission statements are almost always based on the premise that the very purpose of the school is to ensure *all*, not most, students are learning at high levels. Parents of students who are unsuccessful in school and find their schooling to be a negative experience will take no comfort in knowing that most kids are successful. Every school should be committed to providing every student with the same experience and opportunities that the staff would want for their own children.

Second, Jim Collins (2001) in *Good to Great* reminds us that being "good" is the enemy of becoming "great." Being good makes the leader's job of creating a sense of urgency more difficult. But again, if educators recognize the implications for students who are unsuccessful in the K–12 system, they will demonstrate their commitment to learning for every student is driven by a sense of urgency.

A basic tenet of creating a culture of continuous improvement is that regardless of how well an organization is performing on average, there is always room for improvement. Continuous improvement is a journey that never ends. Therefore, it is also important to realize that student performance on state assessments is only one indicator of school effectiveness. Every class and every course has a bottom quartile, and while the aggregate data may reflect student success, examining evidence of learning kid by kid and skill by skill inevitably demonstrates there is always room for improvement.

Another way to respond to this issue of disregarding the PLC process because you are the good-enough school is to ask which part of that process would not benefit all students with the following questions.

- Should we leave the critical issues associated with effective teaching and learning up to individual teachers to resolve, or should we work together collaboratively?

- Should we allow individual teachers to determine the most essential standards and how those standards translate into student work, or should we make these decisions collaboratively?

- Should we leave the questions associated with monitoring each student's learning on a timely basis to each teacher to determine, or does equity require us to address these questions collaboratively?

- Should we leave the question of what to do with students who are struggling with their learning to each teacher to resolve, or should the school create a system of interventions that guarantees students who struggle will receive extra time and support for their learning?

- Should we recognize that the best way to inform and improve our individual and team practice is to analyze collectively ongoing evidence of student learning?

While some educators may question the *work* associated with implementing the PLC process, they rarely question the efficacy of the *individual practices* that reflect a PLC culture—especially if viewed through the lens of what they would want, or expect, for their own children.

Doesn't all this attention to interventions neglect the gifted and talented student?

No. One of the most persistent misconceptions about PLCs is that plans for additional time and support are only for low-achieving students. Leaders of PLCs work to create a culture designed to stretch the aspirations and performance levels of *all* students (and adults too), rather than a select few.

For example, high schools that offer advanced placement courses recognize that students who undertake a more rigorous and challenging curriculum will need additional time and support at certain points in their courses of study. By providing a systematic plan for additional time and support for *all students*, leaders of PLCs create a way to provide assistance to all students within the school day regardless of the teacher to whom they are assigned or the degree of difficulty of their particular course of study.

It is critical not to view the practice of providing additional time and support for students as a deficit model. PLCs do not take attention and learning levels away from one group of students in order to assist others. All students, including the most gifted and talented, will need additional time and support in their learning at one time or another. One of the great ironies of education is that when a student is labeled gifted and talented, we expect that the school should have a plan to do whatever is needed to fulfill the learning potential of the student. When a district provides this sort of attention to all students, it does not take it away from gifted and talented students and give it to students who normally may be less academically capable.

Consider this analogy: If a high school has a rule that only students who weigh two hundred pounds or more can join the football team, the average weight of the football team will be at least two hundred pounds, probably more. But if the school decides to offer the benefits of varsity football to *all students* who would like to participate, even those who weigh less than two hundred pounds, the average weight of the team will decline, but the weight of those students who weigh two hundred pounds or more will not diminish. The same holds true in the academic arena. Providing all students with additional time, support, and extension does not lessen the attention for one group of students, but rather extends best practices to all students.

What do we do when a student is struggling because of misbehavior?

To effectively respond when students struggle due to misbehavior, teachers must apply the same type of collective focus and processes used in a PLC to provide academic interventions. Using the four critical questions of a PLC, a faculty must begin by determining the essential academic and social behaviors that every student must learn to succeed in school. For behavior, teachers should not answer this question independently, but instead collectively as a staff, as these are behaviors that students should demonstrate across the school and as they progress from year to year. Then teachers must systematically teach the standards, instead of just punishing students for not already possessing them. Next, staff must determine which students have mastered these critical behavior outcomes and which students will need additional time and support. At this point, the school is ready to effectively target behavior interventions.

To learn more about how to systematically provide effective behavior interventions, we recommend studying the research behind PBS—positive behavior supports.

Developed by George Sugai, Rob Horner, and their associates, PBS is a proactive, systematic approach for establishing the social culture and individualized behavior supports schools need to be effective learning environments for all students. Specifically, schools identify clear and measurable *outcomes* to improve student behavior and achievement; collect and use *data* to guide their decisions; implement relevant, evidence-based *practices*; and invest in *systems* that will ensure that they implement practices with fidelity and sustain them over time. Like PLC and RTI, PBS is not a program, but a process. It does not endorse or dictate a specific behavior curriculum, assessment product, or intervention program, but instead creates processes that empower site educators to make critical decisions based on the specific learning needs of their students.

How do we make students take responsibility for their own success?

Consider two very different schools. The staff of the first school exhort students to study for tests, complete their homework on time, and persevere if they experience initial difficulty. Alas, some of their students elect to ignore these admonitions. Teachers then impose penalties: failing grades or zeros on missed assignments. In effect, students are free to opt for the penalty rather than do the work. The second school offers no such option. If students do not put sufficient time into their studies, the staff require them to spend time in a tutorial situation. If students do not complete their homework, they progress to an environment where teachers monitor their completion of homework. This school strives to teach students responsibility by insisting they act responsibly—even if under duress—in the hope that students will ultimately internalize the lesson. Which of these schools holds students accountable? Which has enabled irresponsible behavior?

A pyramid of interventions is not the same as saying that students should not experience consequences for lack of effort or irresponsible behavior. It is reasonable to provide students with incentives for completing their work on time and consequences for failing to meet deadlines or achieve the acceptable standard of work. A school that makes learning its primary focus, however, would never consider absolving the student of the responsibility for completing an assignment as an appropriate consequence—particularly if the teacher assumed the assignment would promote student learning.

When schools make working and learning optional, both students and teachers can take the easy way out. Conversely, schools that create an effective system of interventions hold students accountable.

Ensuring Learning

Isn't requiring students to get help and allowing second chances just enabling them? Won't such practices fail to prepare them for college and the real world?

Opponents of systematic intervention use this argument to suggest that requiring students to do what is necessary to succeed in the K–12 system will not prepare them for the sink-or-swim world of higher education or the workplace. But how does allowing students to fail in their education teach them to succeed in their postsecondary lives? We know that students who need remedial courses in order to qualify for entry into higher education are unlikely to ever earn a degree. Failing to help them learn at high levels does not prepare them for college success. We know that students who drop out of high school in the United States pay the highest economic penalty of any industrialized nation. They will earn only thirty-three cents for every dollar a college graduate makes. Their life expectancy will be dramatically shorter. Their own children will be unlikely to ever have access to a college education and are likely to continue the cycle of poverty in their own lives. These are irrefutable facts (Breslow, 2012; Organisation for Economic Co-operation and Development, 2014; Tavernise, 2012). The argument that allowing students to fail in the K–12 system prepares them for postsecondary success clearly has no basis in history, fact, or logic.

The adage that nothing succeeds like success is based on the premise that those with a history of success are likely to meet the next challenge they confront. Graduates of Adlai E. Stevenson High School in Lincolnshire, Illinois, are living proof of that saying. Stevenson students are required to demonstrate responsible behavior. If they do so, they earn increasing privileges as they advance through school. If they do not, the school becomes more and more directive, insisting that they complete their work and do what is necessary to succeed in school. Students learn that good grades and responsible behavior are expected and rewarded and that bad grades and irresponsible behavior lead to a loss of privileges and a closely monitored environment that ensures students put in the effort to succeed in their classwork. This system helped the school reduce its failure rate from 35 percent to 1 percent.

So how have those students fared after leaving Stevenson and facing the challenges of higher education? Each year, the school conducts a survey of all seniors as well as a random sampling of its graduates one and five years after their graduation. The results from the 2014–2015 Adlai E. Stevenson Student Surveys (Martin & Perkins, 2015) are typical.

- One hundred percent of students who completed their first year of college plan to return to college for a second year. The national average is 70 percent.

- Seventy percent felt their academic preparation in high school was superior to that of the other students in their college, 28 percent felt it was the same, and 2 percent felt it was not as good.

- Ninety-seven percent of these college students reported they became more responsible for their own learning as they advanced through high school.

- Ninety percent of the students who entered college upon graduating earned a bachelor's degree within five years. The national average is 39 percent.

If educators want to prepare students for the challenges of the real world, they should teach their students the self-discipline, responsibility, and work ethic that will help them overcome those challenges.

What do we do for interventions when we have tried everything and the student is still failing?

Every school has at least a handful of students who have tremendous needs and for whom it feels it has tried everything. Finding solutions for these students is very hard. This should be expected, for if easily apparent solutions were available, the dedicated educators who have served these students in prior years would have used them.

The power of the PLC process is not in providing the answers to every problem but in creating a collaborative process to lead schools toward the right answers for their students. To this end, we recommend that every school has, as one of its collaborative site teams, a school intervention team. The purpose of this team is to focus intensely on the individual needs of a school's most at-risk students. Because students in need of intensive support usually have multiple needs, it is important that the intervention team comprises site experts in the specific areas that cause students to struggle in school, such as:

- Foundational reading

- Number sense

- Writing

- English language

- Attendance

- Academic and social behaviors

The intervention team should meet frequently, just like any other team in the PLC process. While members of the team might represent a variety of content expertise, the uniting focus of the team is applying the PLC critical questions to each student referred for team consideration.

Ensuring Learning

- What skills or knowledge does *this student* need to learn?
- How will we know if *this student* is learning it?
- How will we respond when *this student* is not learning?
- How will we respond when *this student* is learning?

This collaborative problem-solving approach to intensive interventions is the key to finding the right interventions for a school's most at-risk students.

What programs do you recommend for interventions?

Generally speaking, we are not big fans of purchased intervention programs. We find that many schools and districts fall into the trap of searching for the perfect product to buy that will help all their struggling readers, writers, or mathematics students. Wouldn't it be great if there were a single program a school could buy and every student would learn how to read? If this product existed and was used for core instruction with all students, the school would not need to provide any reading interventions. Unfortunately, this product does not exist. At-risk readers don't all struggle for the same reason, so there is no one program that will address every student's unique needs. We are not suggesting that there are not any effective, scientifically research-based products available that can become powerful, targeted tools in a school's intervention toolbox. But teachers must use these tools in a very targeted, diagnostic way.

In the end, a school will get much better results if staff members spend less time searching for the latest and greatest intervention *program* and more time strengthening their intervention *process*, having teachers work in collaborative teams to find the most effective teaching practices for their students.

What are the district's responsibilities for ensuring every school has systematic interventions?

First and foremost, district leadership must recognize that it is disingenuous to proclaim a mission of high levels of learning for all students and then fail to develop a system to provide additional time and support for students who are not learning. It is the district's responsibility to require each school to collaboratively develop a systematic, sequential plan of interventions for students who are struggling with their learning. Interventions should occur within the school day and regardless of the teacher to whom students are assigned. The plans should be *systematic*—schoolwide plans for all students—and should also reflect other clear criteria. For example, the plans must fulfill the following criteria.

- **Timely:** Not waiting until late in the school year for intervention

- **Directive:** Not merely encouraging or providing an opportunity for students to receive assistance

- **Fluid and flexible:** So students can move in and out of receiving help as needed

- **Monitored:** To address the issue of how the plan will be checked for effectiveness

Additionally, the district has a responsibility to provide the necessary leadership, training, and resources required for the successful development and implementation of effective intervention and extension plans. While district leadership must require each school to develop effective plans, the district has a reciprocal responsibility to provide the training and resources that school leaders will need to fulfill their responsibilities.

Finally, at the heart of every high-performing PLC is the idea that educators learn best from each other and by doing the work. Therefore, district leaders must implement processes and procedures that require school leaders to share their plans with each other—learning about the specific ideas in each other's plans as well as about data regarding the plans' impact on student learning. The district expectation should be that incrementally, over time, student learning data will improve as a result of the continual refinement of each school's plan for additional time, support, and extension.

Ensuring Learning

Additional PLC Resources to Dig Deeper: How Will We Respond When Some Students Don't Learn and When Some Do?

- Buffum, A., Mattos, M., & Weber, C. (2009). *Pyramid response to intervention: RTI, professional learning communities, and how to respond when kids don't learn.* Bloomington, IN: Solution Tree Press.

- Buffum, A., Mattos, M., & Weber, C. (2012). *Simplifying response to intervention: Four essential guiding principles.* Bloomington, IN: Solution Tree Press.

- DuFour, R., DuFour, R., Eaker, R., & Karhanek, G. (2010). *Raising the bar and closing the gap: Whatever it takes.* Bloomington, IN: Solution Tree Press.

Final Thoughts

Educators often tell us that their schools are struggling to become PLCs because they just can't get staff to buy into it. Here is the key to addressing that concern: people become committed to the PLC process when they see it work! Ask almost any teacher what his or her favorite part of the job is, and most will say, "When I see a student 'get it,' especially one who has been struggling." So unless teachers start to see more students succeeding due to their collective efforts, then all the collaboration was nothing more than additional work to achieve the same results they were getting while working in isolation.

A school begins the PLC journey by building the foundation, forming the right teams, and focusing on the first two critical questions of the PLC process.

1. What is it we want our students to learn? What knowledge, skills, and dispositions do we expect them to acquire?

2. How will we know our students are learning? What evidence will we gather to ensure students understand the skills and concepts we are teaching?

It would be extremely difficult to collectively respond when students don't learn if teachers cannot agree on what students have to learn in the first place and if they did not know which students were not learning these essential standards. But we would discourage a school or district from committing years of focus on these foundational steps before beginning to address the last two critical questions.

3. How will we respond when some of our students don't learn?

4. How will we respond when many of our students have already demonstrated proficiency in the skill or concept under consideration?

Instead, teacher teams set short-term SMART goals, unit by unit, on the essential skills and knowledge students must learn for future success. The team can then, on this limited number of learning outcomes, begin to apply all four critical questions. This will provide teacher teams with immediate results on their collaboration, and more important, the PLC process will immediately begin to help students.

Finally, we find that every school currently has interventions, but they tend to not be very systematic, timely, targeted, directive, or effective. Getting started on interventions might not require starting from scratch, but instead might require repurposing and retargeting staff, time, and interventions that you already have in place.

Chapter 6

Defining the District's Role in the PLC Process

In the late 1970s, researchers, writers, and educational leaders began to focus on the instructional behaviors of the classroom teacher as a key factor associated with student learning. This period is often referred to as the era of teacher-effects research. During this time, the focus of researchers shifted from the more personal characteristics of successful teachers to identifying specific teacher behaviors that have a positive correlation with higher levels of student learning (Marzano, Pickering, & Pollock, 2001). During the 1980s, researchers expanded their efforts to address the issue of school effects—the characteristics of highly effective schools and how the culture of individual schools can affect student achievement (Marzano, 2003).

Years of research have validated the fact that the particular teacher a student has, as well as the school a student attends, can have a significant impact on student learning. In more recent years, researchers have extended this logic to the role that district-level leadership plays in student achievement. The findings are clear: what district leaders do—or do not do—has an impact on schools, teachers, and, ultimately, the level of student learning throughout the entire district.

With the increased focus on the importance of district-level leadership, many district leaders have recognized that the concepts and practices of a high-performing PLC offer the best hope to enhance the learning of all students across an entire district. Rather than settling for pockets of achievement in a few good schools sprinkled throughout the district, district leaders have begun to ask, "How can we implement the PLC process throughout our district—not just in all schools but also in every office and at every level?"

Researchers have learned much about successful implementation of the PLC process districtwide. Successful district leaders recognize the need to develop a collaborative culture that is simultaneously tight and loose.

The culture is tight about the fact that high levels of learning for all students is the fundamental purpose of the district—every school, every team, and every classroom.

They initially work with a small guiding coalition of district leaders (including teachers) to gain a deep, rich understanding of PLC processes and practices, along with the relevant vocabulary. As they expand implementation districtwide, they turn their focus to aligning the work throughout the district in ways that are consistent with and support the learning mission.

They capture the power of collaborative teaming by insisting that each school, as well as the district office, organize into collaborative teams. And importantly, they give direction to the work of the teams, frequently monitoring and celebrating progress along the way.

District leaders who have successfully implemented the PLC process also recognize the importance of developing the leadership capacity of principals. They realize that significant, systemic, districtwide change must focus on and enhance the effectiveness of each principal, knowing that it is impossible to create excellent schools throughout the district with weak and ineffective principals.

Effective district leaders recognize their obligation to provide the necessary resources and training to build a culture of continuous improvement in which teams work collaboratively to gain shared knowledge about best practices, engage in action research, and make effective, data-based decisions. And very importantly, the best districts limit initiatives so that educators can focus their efforts and energies on becoming better at the PLC process.

Within these broad parameters, district leaders develop a loose environment in which they encourage and support people, and especially collaborative teams, in their efforts to find creative and innovative ways to enhance student learning and solve problems.

Changing the culture of an entire school district is especially challenging. Bumps in the road, detours, and occasional breakdowns are inevitable. Change, especially cultural change, can lead to confusion and resistance. And each step in the PLC journey generates any number of questions from administrators, teachers, support staff, students, and their parents. The following are some of the most common.

Implementing a Districtwide or Building-Level PLC

Should the central office implement the PLC process throughout all the district schools, or should implementation occur at the building level?

Successful districtwide implementation requires both district- and school-level leadership. The key is to identify those things about which district leadership will be tight, and within those tight parameters promote collaboration, innovation, and ownership—areas in which the district will be loose. (See the introduction to this chapter for a detailed description of what must be tight and what can be loose in a PLC.)

Can the PLC process succeed in a school with a weak or ineffective principal?

One of the most consistent research findings on effective schools is that highly effective schools have highly effective principals (Marzano, 2003). This is often referred to as the "principal principle." Good—even great—things can occur in schools with weak leaders, but the pockets of excellence that exist in almost every school do not translate into high levels of learning across the entire school. Without an effective principal, the various elements of effective schooling practices cannot be brought together, nurtured, or maintained on a schoolwide basis.

The most effective district leaders realize that if they are to succeed in implementing PLC processes and practices in a way that results in significant and systemic gains in student learning, they must focus on the role of the building principal—individually, but equally important, as a member of the team.

There are few things that take higher priority for central office leaders in high-performing districts than developing the capacity of each principal and the ability of the principals to work as a high-performing team—a team in which members work together, learn together, share with each other, and hold each other mutually accountable. A principal in a PLC moves from thinking he or she is only responsible for improving the learning levels of *his or her kids* to realizing he or she plays an integral role in and has a responsibility to positively impact the learning of *all students* within the district.

Supporting and Monitoring a Districtwide PLC Initiative

How can the central office best support a districtwide PLC initiative?

The central office plays a vital role in supporting the effective implementation of the PLC process by constantly and consistently bringing clarity to the work. Simply put, one workshop, book study, or visit from a consultant will not suffice. The district office must keep reminding everyone of "why we are doing this work in the first place," constantly reminding people that the goal is not to become a PLC; the goal is to significantly enhance the learning of all students throughout the district—in every school and in every classroom, student by student and skill by skill. The PLC process is a *means* to that end, *not the end in itself.*

Beyond emphasizing the why of the work, the district can enhance clarity by reinforcing a clear understanding of what high-performing PLCs are, what they look like, how they work, and how PLC practices, if done well and with fidelity, can enhance student learning levels across the district and lead to a more professional and personally satisfying workplace for adults. In this regard, district leaders work relentlessly to create and reinforce a common vocabulary and a deep, rich understanding of the essential processes and practices reflective of a high-performing PLC.

District leaders must recognize that deep, rich understanding comes only from deep learning, and deep learning comes from meaningful doing. One of the most significant ways the central office can support the implementation of PLC practices is by being clear about the work that must be done and why it must be done. Central office leaders identify specific tasks and processes that can have a positive impact on student learning. They then provide the necessary support, resources, training, and examples to administrators, faculty, and support staff in an effective and timely manner.

Deep, rich learning also comes from learning from each other—doing the right work together. District leaders recognize that the PLC process will not have its greatest impact if they merely replace isolated classrooms with isolated schools, so they create processes to ensure schools can learn from one another. Central office leaders ask principals to work together to anticipate issues and questions, share team-developed products, practice and rehearse the work they undertake, and, very importantly, share evidence of student learning. A culture of collaboration, transparency, and shared learning is at the heart and soul of a district that functions as a true PLC, and it takes effective district leadership to create that culture.

Just as students learn at different rates, so do adults. Therefore, district leaders realize that some schools, teams, and individuals will need more and perhaps different support than others. District leaders recognize that formative assessment is not just for students, so they create systems to monitor the work of adults along the way, providing additional time and support—and encouragement—when and where necessary. Effective district leaders are masters of differentiated leadership.

And, just like students, adults need appreciation and recognition for their hard work and the improvements they make. Effective district leaders understand that the very nature of continuous improvement implies that there is no end to the effort. It is a journey without a destination. They sustain the improvement process by creating small wins and recognizing and celebrating them when they occur. Rather than relying solely on big celebrations that occur annually, if ever, district leaders recognize the exemplary work of individuals and teams when it occurs. Effective districts recognize there is a big difference between hoping for small wins and planning for small wins.

How can the central office monitor progress in a districtwide PLC initiative?

District office leaders must recognize that they can most effectively monitor progress by closely associating and involving themselves with the work—day in and day out. The most effective monitoring is not an event but a way of life in a district that functions as a PLC. District leaders must capture the power of formative assessment and monitor the ongoing work of adults, just as teacher teams monitor the ongoing learning of their students.

One of the most effective ways to monitor the ongoing work that occurs across the district is by examining products that teams produce. Leaders must review the quality of the products in comparison to collaboratively developed standards of quality. The most effective monitoring of products occurs not only when district office personnel review them but when principals and teachers share openly with their colleagues as a way to enhance adult learning and effectiveness.

District leaders must also recognize that effective leaders are obsessed with results—are the students learning, and how do we know? District leaders embed the use of formative assessments at all levels across the district. While the results of teacher-made formative assessments are primarily for the use of the teacher teams, district leaders can also reap the benefits of these formative assessments. If district leaders work closely with principals and teachers, and if principals share learning data with each other and with district leaders on a timely and regular basis, district leaders can grasp the learning levels that occur within each school and within each team as the year progresses.

Additionally, district leaders monitor progress through the use of a few periodic, districtwide benchmark assessments. These assessments are not in lieu of the formative assessments developed by teacher teams, but a useful addition—another lens through which to look. And, increasingly, districts conduct an annual school review, in which each school presents a data portrait that represents the level of progress it has made in each grade by each subgroup, and in key subject areas or courses. The best school data reviews are highly interactive with everyone engaged in asking questions, clarifying the work they undertook, sharing difficulties, and including ideas about how to improve results in specific areas.

Each chapter in *Learning by Doing, Third Edition* (DuFour et al., 2016), contains a Professional Learning Communities at Work Continuum—a rubric for collaborative self-reflection regarding the implementation progress of the PLC process and practices. The appendix of *Every School, Every Team, Every Classroom: District Leadership for Growing Professional Learning Communities at Work* (Eaker & Keating, 2012) contains a survey along with a format for an annual report schools make each year to the White River Board of Education in Buckley, Washington. Solution Tree (www.solution-tree.com) provides an additional resource for monitoring progress. This service consists of an in-depth, on-site visit, interviews, and reviews of products, resulting in a detailed summary that not only reports progress but points to specific next steps.

Additional PLC Resources to Dig Deeper: Defining the District's Role in the PLC Process

- DuFour, R., DuFour, R., & Eaker, R. (2008). *Revisiting Professional Learning Communities at Work: New insights for improving schools.* Bloomington, IN: Solution Tree Press.

- DuFour, R., & Fullan, M. (2013). *Cultures built to last: Systemic PLCs at Work.* Bloomington, IN: Solution Tree Press.

Final Thoughts

In recent years, the important role the district office can play in enhancing student learning has received considerable attention. Changing district culture, however, is difficult, complex, and incremental work. Implementing PLC processes and practices requires strong, passionate, and persistent district-level leadership that collaboratively addresses key questions such as, What are our priorities? What are the specific conditions we expect to see in every school? What must we do to build the capacity of people throughout the organization to create these conditions? What indicators of progress will we monitor? and What district practices and leadership behaviors are not aligned with the purpose and priorities we have articulated?

The questions addressed in this chapter represent those that most frequently emerge among school leaders. Responding to questions is a way of life for district-level leaders, and how well district leaders anticipate and respond to questions goes a long way in determining the pace and success of reculturing a district into a high-performing PLC.

Chapter 7

Addressing Consensus and Conflict in a PLC

The PLC process works best when educators spend some time learning together about both the rationale for and key elements of the process. "Focus on *why* before *how*" is one of the mantras of the consensus-building process. Building consensus requires more than merely averaging opinions. It requires building shared knowledge among the entire staff on both the current reality of the school and the evidence of best practice in our field. Ask uninformed people to make decisions, and the end result is uninformed decisions. So the initial challenge in achieving consensus is building shared knowledge among the entire staff. We have found that when people of goodwill have access to the same information when making a decision, they are likely to arrive at similar conclusions. Building consensus does not eliminate conflict, but it offers a solid framework for dealing with conflict.

Responding to Conflict

Do we need everyone to buy into the PLC process before we begin implementation?

No. There is a difference between consensus and unanimity. The staff might strive for unanimity but will probably have to settle for consensus. If everyone on the staff must agree in order for the school to initiate change, if each person has veto power, the school is certain to languish in stagnation.

We offer the following definition of *consensus* that serves as a more reasonable standard for moving forward. We have consensus when all points of view have been not only heard but also solicited and the will of the group becomes evident even to those who most oppose it. We offer a detailed process for meeting these standards in chapter 9 of *Learning by Doing, Third Edition* (DuFour et al., 2016).

When will we know we have consensus?

A group reaches consensus when all points of view have been heard and the will of the group is evident even to those who most oppose it.

Is it okay to start the PLC process with just the teachers and teams who want to do it?

It is highly preferable to implement the PLC process on a schoolwide basis rather than only with a few teams or with those who want to engage in PLC practices. There are decisions that can only be made at the school level. For example, individual teachers or even teams of teachers cannot change the school schedule to allow time for team meetings or to provide students with additional time, support, or extension. Individuals and teams do not have control of the school budget; hence, the allocation of resources for such things as training requires a schoolwide approach. In short, successfully undertaking the structural and cultural changes necessary to function as a high-performing PLC requires broader systematic and systemic changes that individual teachers or teacher teams cannot provide.

Beyond the practical issues related to implementation of PLC processes and practices, there is a fundamental ethical question that schools must address: Should individual teachers or teams have the freedom and autonomy to opt out of practices that have proven to be highly successful in enhancing student learning? Many of the classroom practices that hinder student success happen because the school allows them to happen. In a school culture that reflects PLC processes and practices, everyone is *expected* to work collaboratively to seek and implement best practices in order to demonstrate continuous improvement. Opting out of best practice should not be an option. (In fact, in most professions, doing so would be considered *malpractice!*)

However, we should recognize that there are schools in which the school leadership has shown little or no interest in implementing PLC processes and practices. In these cases, it is preferable for an individual team to work within its sphere of influence to implement the processes and practices to the best of its ability. While they will be limited in their work, team members can have a positive impact on their students by collaboratively focusing on the critical questions of learning.

There may also be the added benefit of "influencing upward." That is, as an individual team demonstrates improved student learning by doing the work of a PLC, other teams—and maybe even the principal—will begin to take notice and see the value of working as a PLC. There are many examples of schoolwide change that began with an individual team. So do not underestimate the power of starting small.

What if we have a colleague who is unwilling to engage in the PLC process?

Once again, the PLC process requires a culture that is simultaneously loose and tight. *Tight* means that some things in the school are nondiscretionary. Everyone must observe what is tight, and if someone fails to, leaders will direct him or her to do so. For example, in virtually every school, teachers are required to turn in grades at the end of the grading period. A teacher who fails to turn in grades will be directed to do so. If the teacher continues to refuse to turn in grades, he or she is considered insubordinate and subject to increasingly severe penalties—a letter of reprimand, suspension, and ultimately dismissal—because notifying students and their parents of student progress is a fundamental responsibility of a teacher. Most teachers would not even consider the possibility of refusing to assign grades.

When a school functions as a PLC, working with colleagues on the key elements of the PLC process is a core responsibility of each teacher. Continued failure to work with colleagues or to observe the process must result in a written directive detailing the specific behaviors the teacher must exhibit and making it clear that continued failure to demonstrate those behaviors will result in specific repercussions for insubordination.

How can we persuade someone to change his or her attitude?

Assume good intentions on the part of the resistant person, and ask that person to explain his or her concerns. Seek common ground. If the person continues to resist acting in accordance with decisions made by consensus, you can use Howard Gardner's strategies for changing someone's mind. Those strategies include:

1. Reasoning and rationale thinking

2. Research

3. Resonance

4. Representational redescription

5. Resources and rewards

6. Real-world events

7. Requirements

(See chapter 9 of *Learning by Doing, Third Edition* [DuFour et al., 2016], for a detailed description of Gardner's strategies.)

If these strategies fail to convince the reluctant staff member to participate in the process, the final step is for the principal to require that the teacher engage in the process and stipulate consequences if he or she fails to do so. From that point on, the principal should monitor the behavior of the teacher, rather than how happy or unhappy he or she is about engaging in the behavior. If the person engages in new behavior and it leads to a consistently new and better experience, the teacher changes his or her own attitude. Changes in beliefs are typically the result of changes in experience, which in turn can only be brought about by changes in behavior.

What if our principal won't hold people accountable to their team norms or to the PLC process?

We should view the issue of principals not holding people accountable for violations of team norms or failure to implement the PLC process through two lenses: from a team perspective and from a district office perspective. A school will not be successful if some do not honor the norms, or if not everyone implements the PLC processes and practices. Shared commitment and mutual accountability are the glue that holds a culture of continuous improvement together.

From a team perspective, it is important that teams address the issue of accountability by their members as they develop norms. Each team should have a specific norm that addresses the question, What will happen if a team member violates one or more of our norms?

This is an important step because it creates a sequential protocol for the team to follow. For example, the first step in the plan might be for the team leader to address the issue with the team member. The second step may be for the team as a whole to meet with the team member who is not adhering to the team norms. If these steps fail, the protocol might call for the team leader or the entire team to meet with the principal for recommendations about how to proceed. At this point, it is imperative that the principal addresses the issue by directing the offending individual to demonstrate specific behaviors. Ignoring an obvious problem quickly destroys a leader's credibility. But principals will be reluctant to confront those problems unless they are certain the central office will support their efforts.

The central office must also hold principals accountable for implementing PLC practices with fidelity and mutual accountability. One way to promote this accountability is by creating a team approach to the principalship in which each principal shares both the work of teams and evidence of student learning with his or her colleagues and the central office staff on a regular basis. This transparency makes any team dysfunction evident.

The district-level culture should also be one of mutual support. Principals should feel comfortable stating to their fellow principals, or to the appropriate district office person, that they are having a problem with a teacher or two and could use some help in addressing the problem.

Leaders must not ignore issues stemming from the violation of team norms or failure to engage in the essential work. The unwillingness of leaders to address people who violate their commitments or the key elements of the process dooms the implementation of the PLC process, since it sends the message to everyone that this collaborative PLC work isn't really that important after all.

Providing Support

We get it, but our principal does not. What can we do?

The people who are most effective and satisfied in any job have the ability to influence up; that is, they know they can impact the thinking of those to whom they report. If a team of teachers "gets" the PLC process and the principal does not, the team has both an opportunity and obligation to help the principal better understand the process.

The key to influencing up is to propose a partnership to improve the school rather than offer a critique of all the principal's deficiencies. The team members should begin by assuming good intentions on the part of the principal and believing that adults, even principals, can learn to become more effective if they have access to relevant information and support.

For example, a team of teachers could ask the principal to set aside some time to discuss ideas for improving the school and provide the principal with preliminary information and research on the potential benefits of the PLC process.

During that meeting, members could take the following actions.

- Explain why they have concluded that the PLC process would be a powerful way to improve student achievement

- Offer to help lead and support the process by accepting responsibility for:

  - Responding to faculty questions and concerns about the PLC process

  - Building consensus for the process with faculty

  - Serving as a guiding coalition to help oversee implementation

Addressing
Conflict

- Developing sample schedules that would provide time for teacher collaboration and systematic intervention and enrichment for students

The team could then identify specific behaviors from the principal that would be essential to successful implementation. For example, the team could ask if the principal would be willing to:

- Provide sacred time for team collaboration
- Establish a process to clarify and monitor the work of collaborative teams
- Support the creation of systematic intervention and enrichment processes
- Protect the school from other improvement initiatives while implementing the PLC process
- Hold all teachers accountable to the process and to the commitments they make to their colleagues

A team of teacher leaders should initiate this conversation rather than an individual, and it may require more than one meeting. But if teachers demonstrate a sincere interest in improving their school, offer to play a leadership role in implementing an improvement plan, clarify how they will support the process, and help the principal understand how he or she can contribute to its success, they can be a powerful force for good in their schools. In order for this to happen, they must acknowledge their ability to help shape the culture of their school and resist the temptation to feign helplessness.

How can teams plan for celebration in the PLC process?

The SMART goal aspect of PLCs provides the opportunity for frequent celebrations if teams break annual SMART goals down into short-term goals for units. For example, team members might set a goal to have at least 80 percent of their students demonstrate proficiency on a common formative assessment at the end of their first unit of instruction. If they achieve that goal, they should celebrate. If they are unable to achieve the goal, but discover that a particular skill or concept was problematic for students and then identify and implement a strategy to address the problem successfully, they should celebrate! As the year progresses, if students who initially struggled begin to demonstrate proficiency on a regular basis, the team should celebrate! Furthermore, the goal setting and celebration can extend into individual classrooms and include students in the process. When a class achieves a clearly defined goal, the teacher should lead it in celebration.

Celebration is an important part of sustaining any continuous improvement process. We offer specific criteria for celebrations in chapter 9 of *Learning by Doing, Third Edition* (DuFour et al., 2016).

How long does it take to become a PLC?

A number of factors influence how long it takes to implement the structural and cultural changes involved in becoming a PLC. The commitment, passion, and persistence of district- and school-level leaders affect the pace of change, as does the quality of collaboration and professional development, just to name a few factors. We have found that elementary schools are able to change more quickly than high schools, yet there are examples of high schools attaining improved results quickly. We can say the same about school size. While smaller schools would seem easier to change, there are many examples of larger schools that have fully embedded PLC practices rather quickly.

Many schools see significant improvement after one year of embedding PLC processes and practices. Others take longer. A realistic expectation after one year is for the basic structures and the initial work associated with a PLC to be in place and for teacher teams to be producing products such as curriculum guides that emphasize the essential standards and commonly developed formative assessments. And importantly, the school should have developed a plan to provide students with additional time, support, and extension within the school day regardless of the teacher to whom they are assigned.

By the end of the second year, a typical school can expect to fully refine the processes and practices of a PLC. While the emphasis in year one was on getting started, the emphasis in year two, and every year thereafter, should be on getting better. You will know that you are making progress when the school is characterized by specificity regarding essential learnings—team by team, task by task, kid by kid, skill by skill—and *fidelity*, with faculty and staff doing the work because they believe it is the right thing to do, as opposed to doing the work out of compliance. While improvement in student achievement may appear during the early stages of implementation, especially in a few specific subjects or courses, by the end of the third year, you should see widespread gains in student learning.

Additional PLC Resources to Dig Deeper: Addressing Consensus and Conflict in a PLC

**Additional PLC Resources to Dig Deeper:
Addressing Concensus and Conflict in a PLC**

- DuFour, R., & DuFour, R. (2011). *Leading difficult conversations* [DVD]. Bloomington, IN: Solution Tree Press.

- DuFour, R., DuFour, R., Eaker, R., Many, T. W., & Mattos, M. (2016). *Learning by doing: A handbook for Professional Learning Communities at Work* (3rd ed.). Bloomington, IN: Solution Tree Press.

Final Thoughts

This chapter brings us full circle back to the first chapter on the importance of building a solid foundation for a PLC—including a shared purpose for the school, a shared vision of what the school is attempting to become in order to fulfill that purpose, shared collective commitments of what each individual staff member can do to help move the school toward the vision, and shared goals to serve as targets and timelines for monitoring progress toward the vision. The key word in each instance is *shared*. With this solid foundation in place, every member of the staff has the moral authority to ask others to act in accordance with the agreed-on foundation of their school. When the entire staff promotes and protects the purpose, vision, commitments, and goals of the school, the PLC process becomes a collective endeavor fueled by a common mission and direction. Those who have experienced this collective endeavor as members of high-performing PLCs would never choose to return to working in isolation.

Afterword

It's a Journey, Not a Destination

Reculturing schools and school districts into high-performing PLCs is a difficult and complex journey. While there is no one way to proceed on the journey, there are certain steps—stops along the way—that schools must address. Educators must work to create and truly embrace a clear and compelling purpose—a focus on high levels of learning for students. They must clarify and add meaning to the critical questions associated with student learning and develop a systematic plan to provide additional time, support, and extension for students within the school day. They must address each of these steps by developing a collaborative culture through the use of high-performing collaborative teams. And, ultimately, educators must work to establish a relentless focus on results by constantly asking, "Are the students learning, and how do we know?"

Addressing each of these steps will likely cause some degree of apprehension and confusion and will most certainly generate a number of questions. The degree to which educators can anticipate these questions and then engage one another in answering them will go a long way in determining the pace and smoothness of implementing the practices reflective of a PLC. The process of posing questions and searching together for answers—some of them simple and many of them complex—is a vital tool for any learning organization, especially schools and school districts.

We recognize that questions can arise from a variety of motives—an attempt to clarify information, deepen understanding, profess a belief, or oppose a proposition. Regardless of the motive, educators must learn to listen deeply, seek to understand, assume good intentions on the part of the questioner, and steadfastly resist the temptation to vilify those who question them. When handled well, questions present a wonderful opportunity to build shared knowledge.

A Compendium of Experience, Not a Fountain of Wisdom

The story is told of a young man seeking advice from Mark Twain on how to be successful. Twain told the man that the key to success was making good decisions.

The young man then asked how one learns to make good decisions. Twain gave a two-word answer: "Through experience." Finally, the young man asked how he could gain this valuable experience. Twain responded, "By making bad decisions." Whether you are embarking on the journey to become a PLC or you have initiated the journey but have gotten bogged down along the way, take comfort in knowing that you are not the first to travel this path. Many of your fellow educators have valuable experience in considering the same questions you will confront, and very often, that experience came from making some bad decisions. Eleanor Roosevelt once advised, "Learn from the mistakes of others. You can't live long enough to make them all yourself." So consider this book not an index of correct answers but rather a compendium of experience—advice from colleagues who have taken the journey before you.

Even with support, however, don't expect the PLC journey to proceed without missteps and mistakes. Even a bad decision can advance your journey if you view it as a learning experience—an opportunity to begin again more intelligently—rather than evidence of inevitable failure.

Perhaps the ultimate question every educator must consider is one that has confronted each generation since time immemorial: "Am I willing to accept things as they are, or am I willing to dig deep and work with others to make the world a better place?" In this context, successfully posing and addressing questions at each step along the PLC journey is simply part of getting started and getting better and better—in other words, *learning by doing*. Get on with it!

References and Resources

Adlai E. Stevenson High School. (n.d.a). *Board of education vision statement.* Accessed at www.d125.org/about/school-board/district-125-board-of-education-vision -statement on October 1, 2015.

Adlai E. Stevenson High School. (n.d.b). *Collective commitments board and admin team.* Accessed at www.d125.org/about/vision/collective-commitments-board-and -admin-team on October 1, 2015.

Adlai E. Stevenson High School. (n.d.c). *Collective commitments faculty.* Accessed at www.d125.org/about/vision/collective-commitments-faculty on October 1, 2015.

Adlai E. Stevenson High School. (n.d.d). *Collective commitments parents.* Accessed at www.d125.org/about/vision/collective-commitments-parents on October 1, 2015.

Adlai E. Stevenson High School. (n.d.e). *Collective commitments students.* Accessed at www.d125.org/about/vision/collective-commitments-students on October 1, 2015.

Adlai E. Stevenson High School. (n.d.f). *Collective commitments support staff.* Accessed at www.d125.org/about/vision/collective-commitments-support-staff on October 1, 2015.

Ainsworth, L. (2013). *"Unwrapping" the standards: A simple process to make standards manageable.* Englewood, CO: Lead + Learn Press.

Ainsworth, L. (2013). *Prioritizing the Common Core: Identifying specific standards to emphasize the most.* Englewood, CO: Lead + Learn Press.

Ainsworth, L. (2015, February 24). *Priority standards: The power of focus* [Blog post]. Accessed at http://blogs.edweek.org/edweek/finding_common_ground/2015/02 /priority_standards_the_power_of_focus.html?qs=larry+ainsworth on December 30, 2015.

American Association of School Librarians. (2009). *Empowering learners: Guidelines for school library programs.* Chicago: Author.

American Institutes for Research & SRI International. (2005, April). *Creating cultures for learning: Supportive relationships in new and redesigned high schools.* Seattle: Bill and Melinda Gates Foundation. Accessed at https://docs.gatesfoundation.org /documents/relationship%20rpt%2010_21.pdf on December 30, 2015.

American Institutes for Research & SRI International. (2006, August). *Evaluation of the Bill and Melinda Gates Foundation's High School Grants Initiative, 2001–2005 final report*. Seattle: Bill and Melinda Gates Foundation. Accessed at https://docs .gatesfoundation.org/Documents/Year4EvaluationAIRSRI.pdf on September 30, 2015.

Bailey, K., & Jakicic, C. (2012). *Common formative assessment: A toolkit for Professional Learning Communities at Work*. Bloomington, IN: Solution Tree Press.

Bailey, K., Jakicic, C., & Spiller, J. (2014). *Collaborating for success with the Common Core: A toolkit for Professional Learning Communities at Work*. Bloomington, IN: Solution Tree Press.

Breslow, J. M. (2012, September 21). *By the numbers: Dropping out of high school*. Accessed at www.pbs.org/wgbh/pages/frontline/education/dropout-nation/by-the -numbers-dropping-out-of-high-school on September 21, 2012.

Buffum, A., & Mattos, M. (Eds.). (2015). *It's about time: Planning interventions and extensions in elementary school*. Bloomington, IN: Solution Tree Press.

Buffum, A., Mattos, M., & Weber, C. (2009). *Pyramid response to intervention: RTI, professional learning communities, and how to respond when kids don't learn*. Bloomington, IN: Solution Tree Press.

Buffum, A., Mattos, M., & Weber, C. (2012). *Simplifying response to intervention: Four essential guiding principles*. Bloomington, IN: Solution Tree Press.

Buffum, A., Mattos, M., & Weber, C. (2013). *RTI at Work Coaching Academy binder*. Bloomington, IN: Solution Tree Press.

Center for Public Education. (2011). *Back to school: How parent involvement affects student achievement*. Accessed at www.centerforpubliceducation.org/Main-Menu /Public-education/Parent-Involvement/Parent-Involvement.html on December 30, 2015.

Collins, J. (2001). *Good to great: Why some companies make the leap . . . and others don't*. New York: HarperBusiness.

Collins, J., & Porras, J. I. (1997). *Built to last: Successful habits of visionary companies*. New York: HarperBusiness.

Community Consolidated School District 54. (2015). *Ensuring student success*. Accessed at http://sd54.org/board/files/2010/04/Mission-Vision-Commitments-and-Goals -English-7-1-151.pdf on October 1, 2015.

Conley, D. T. (2007, March). *Redefining college readiness*. Eugene, OR: Educational Policy Improvement Center.

Deinhart, J. (2015, July 29). *To ability group or not to ability group? That is the question* [Blog post]. Accessed at www.allthingsplc.info/blog/view/303/to-ability-group-or -not-to-ability-group-that-is-the-question on October 1, 2015.

Diament, M. (2014, April 29). *Graduation rates fall short for students with disabilities*. Accessed at www.disabilityscoop.com/2014/04/29/graduation-rates-disabilities /19317 on January 3, 2016.

DuFour, R. (2011). Work together: But only if you want to. *Phi Delta Kappan, 92*(5), 57–61.

DuFour, R., DuFour, R., & Eaker, R. (2008). *Revisiting Professional Learning Communities at Work: New insights for improving schools.* Bloomington, IN: Solution Tree Press.

DuFour, R., DuFour, R., Eaker, R., & Karhanek, G. (2010). *Raising the bar and closing the gap: Whatever it takes.* Bloomington, IN: Solution Tree Press.

DuFour, R., DuFour, R., Eaker, R., & Many, T. W. (2010). *Learning by doing: A handbook for Professional Learning Communities at Work* (2nd ed.). Bloomington, IN: Solution Tree Press.

DuFour, R., DuFour, R., Eaker, R., Many, T. W., & Mattos, M. (2016). *Learning by doing: A handbook for Professional Learning Communities at Work* (3rd ed.). Bloomington, IN: Solution Tree Press.

DuFour, R., & Eaker, R. (1998). *Professional Learning Communities at Work: Best practices for enhancing student achievement.* Bloomington, IN: Solution Tree Press.

DuFour, R., & Fullan, M. (2013). *Cultures built to last: Systemic PLCs at Work.* Bloomington, IN: Solution Tree Press.

DuFour, R., & Reason, C. (2016). *Professional Learning Communities at Work and virtual collaboration: On the tipping point of transformation.* Bloomington, IN: Solution Tree Press.

Eaker, R., & Keating, J. (2012). *Every school, every team, every classroom: District leadership for growing Professional Learning Communities at Work.* Bloomington, IN: Solution Tree Press.

Eaker, R., & Keating, J. (2015). *Kid by kid, skill by skill: Teaching in a Professional Learning Community at Work.* Bloomington, IN: Solution Tree Press.

Easton, L. B. (2009). *Protocols for professional learning.* Alexandria, VA: Association for Supervision and Curriculum Development.

Elmore, R. F. (2003). *School reform from the inside out: Policy, practice, and performance.* Boston: Harvard Education Press.

Epstein, J. L. (2005, September). *Developing and sustaining research-based programs of school, family, and community partnerships: Summary of five years of National Network of Partnership Schools research.* Accessed at www.csos.jhu.edu/P2000/pdf/Research%20Summary.pdf on December 30, 2015.

Erkens, C. (2016). *Collaborative common assessments: Teamwork. Instruction. Results.* Bloomington, IN: Solution Tree Press.

Erkens, C., Jakicic, C., Jessie, L. G., King, D., Kramer, S. V., Many, T. W., et al. (2008). *The collaborative teacher: Working together as a professional learning community.* Bloomington, IN: Solution Tree Press.

Ferriter, W. M., Graham, P., & Wight, M. (2013). *Making teamwork meaningful: Leading progress-driven collaboration in a PLC at Work.* Bloomington, IN: Solution Tree Press.

Gerstner, L. V., Jr. (with Semerad, R. D., Doyle, D. P., & Johnston, W. B.). (1995). *Reinventing education: Entrepreneurship in America's public schools.* New York: Penguin.

Goodlad, J. I. (1983). A study of schooling: Some implications for school improvement. *Phi Delta Kappan, 64*(8), 552–558.

Hansen, A. (2015). *How to develop PLCs for singletons and small schools.* Bloomington, IN: Solution Tree Press.

Hattie, J. (2009). *Visible learning: A synthesis of over 800 meta-analyses relating to achievement.* New York: Routledge.

Hattie, J. (2012). *Visible learning for teachers: Maximizing impact on learning.* New York: Routledge.

Kegan, R., & Lahey, L. L. (2001). *How the way we talk can change the way we work: Seven languages for transformation.* San Francisco: Jossey-Bass.

Lickona, T. (2004). *Character matters: How to help our children develop good judgment, integrity, and other essential virtues.* New York: Touchstone.

Many, T. W., & Horrell, T. (2014, January/February). *Prioritizing the standards using R.E.A.L. criteria.* Accessed at http://c.ymcdn.com/sites/www.tepsa.org /resource/resmgr/imported/Resources/many-realcriteria.pdf on January 4, 2016.

Martin, P., & Perkins, L. (2015, November). *Adlai E. Stevenson High School student surveys 2014–2015.* Accessed at www.d125.org/docs/default-source/documents /student-surveys/2015-student-survey.pdf?sfvrsn=2survey on December 30, 2015.

Marzano, R. J. (2003). *What works in schools: Translating research into action.* Alexandria, VA: Association for Supervision and Curriculum Development.

Marzano, R. J., Pickering, D. J., & Pollock, J. E. (2001). *Classroom instruction that works: Research-based strategies for increasing student achievement.* Alexandria, VA: Association for Supervision and Curriculum Development.

Mason Crest Elementary School. (n.d.). *Mission, vision, collective commitments, and goals.* Accessed at www.fcps.edu/masoncrestes/about/missionVision.html on October 1, 2015.

Mattos, M., & Buffum, A. (Eds.). (2015). *It's about time: Planning interventions and extensions in secondary school.* Bloomington, IN: Solution Tree Press.

Mehta, J. (2013). Why American education fails: And how lessons from abroad could improve it. *Foreign Affairs, 92*(3). Accessed at www.foreignaffairs.com/articles /united-states/2013-04-03/why-american-education-fails on December 30, 2015.

Muhammad, A. (2009). *Transforming school culture: How to overcome staff division.* Bloomington, IN: Solution Tree Press.

National Assessment of Educational Progress. (n.d.). *NAEP questions tool.* Accessed at http://nces.ed.gov/nationsreportcard/itmrlsx on October 1, 2015.

National Education Association. (n.d.). *Research spotlight on academic ability grouping: NEA reviews of the research on best practices in education.* Accessed at www.nea.org /tools/16899.htm on October 1, 2015.

O'Neill, J., & Conzemius, A. (2006). *The power of SMART goals: Using goals to improve student learning.* Bloomington, IN: Solution Tree Press.

Organisation for Economic Co-operation and Development. (2014). *Education at a glance.* Accessed at www.oecd.org/edu/United%20States-EAG2014-Country -Note.pdf on December 12, 2015.

Partnership for 21st Century Learning. (n.d.). *Framework for 21st century learning.* Accessed at www.p21.org/our-work/p21-framework on September 30, 2015.

Reeves, D. (2002). *The leader's guide to standards: A blueprint for educational equity and excellence.* San Francisco: Jossey-Bass.

Reeves, D. (Ed.). (2007). *Ahead of the curve: The power of assessment to transform teaching and learning.* Bloomington, IN: Solution Tree Press.

Samuels, C. A. (2010). Learning-disabled enrollment dips after long climb. *Education Week, 30*(3), 1, 14–15.

Saphier, J., King, M., & D'Auria, J. (2006). Three strands form strong school leadership. *Journal of Staff Development, 27*(2), 51–57.

Saunders, W. C., Goldenberg, C. N., & Gallimore, R. (2009). Increasing achievement by focusing grade-level teams on improving classroom learning: A prospective, quasi-experimental study of Title I schools. *American Educational Research Journal, 46*(4), 1006–1033.

Sparks, S. K., & Many, T. W. (2015). *How to cultivate collaboration in a PLC.* Bloomington, IN: Solution Tree Press.

Stark, P., Noel, A. M., & McFarland, J. (2015, June). *Trends in high school dropout and completion rates in the United States: 1972–2012* (NCES 2015–015). Washington, DC: National Center for Education Statistics.

Tavernise, S. (2012, February 9). Education gap grows between rich and poor, studies say. *New York Times.* Accessed at www.nytimes.com/2012/02/10 /education/education-gap-grows-between-rich-and-poor-studies-show.html on February 30, 2012.

Thimmesh, C. (2006). *Team moon: How 400,000 people landed* Apollo 11 *on the moon.* New York: Houghton Mifflin.

U.S. Department of Education. (1995). *An invitation to your community: Building community partnerships for learning.* Washington, DC: U.S. Government Printing Office.

Wei, R. C., Darling-Hammond, L., Andree, A., Richardson, N., & Orphanos, S. (2009, February). *Professional learning in the learning profession: A status report on teacher development in the U.S. and abroad.* Dallas, TX: National Staff Development Council.

West, M. R. (2012, August). *Is retaining students in the early grades self-defeating?* (CCF Brief No. 49). Washington, DC: Brookings Institution.

Wiliam, D. (2011). *Embedded formative assessment.* Bloomington, IN: Solution Tree Press.

Index

Learning by Doing, Third Edition
Richard DuFour, Rebecca DuFour, Robert Eaker, Thomas W. Many, and Mike Mattos

Discover how to transform your school or district into a high-performing PLC. The third edition of this comprehensive action guide offers new strategies for addressing critical PLC topics, including hiring and retaining new staff, creating team-developed common formative assessments, and more.

BKF746

Solutions for Professional Learning Communities series

These how-to guides—authored by renowned PLC experts—are packed with user-friendly solutions for you and your team. You'll discover practical, research-based strategies for committing to districtwide implementation and explore tools and techniques for monitoring progress to ensure far-reaching, lasting results.

BKF675, BKF668, BKF667, BKF676, BKF678, BKF665

Leading Difficult Conversations
Featuring Richard DuFour and Rebecca DuFour

Gain strategies for addressing the conflicts that can result from transforming a school into a professional learning community. Learn how to hold conversations that lead staff to understand that best practice is to work collaboratively and collectively in high-performing teams.

DVF047

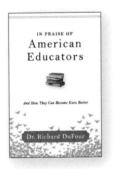

In Praise of American Educators
Richard DuFour

Explore the state of education today. The author establishes why contemporary American educators are the greatest generation in history and then presents specific steps policymakers and educators must take to transform American schools to meet student needs in the 21st century.

BKF702

"Tremendous, tremendous, tremendous!

The speaker made me do some very deep internal reflection about the **PLC process** and the personal responsibility I have in making the school improvement process work **for ALL kids.**"

—Marc Rodriguez, teacher effectiveness coach, Denver Public Schools, Colorado

🤝 PD Services

Our experts draw from decades of research and their own experiences to bring you practical strategies for building and sustaining a high-performing PLC. You can choose from a range of customizable services, from a one-day overview to a multiyear process.

Book your PLC PD today!
888.763.9045

Solution Tree